D1242153

Hopes and Fears of the American People

POTOMAC ASSOCIATES is a nonpartisan research and analysis organization which seeks to encourage lively inquiry into critical issues of public policy. Its purpose is to heighten public understanding and improve public discourse on significant contemporary problems, national and international.

POTOMAC ASSOCIATES provides a forum for distinctive points of view by commissioning brief, timely studies and occasional papers by outstanding authorities in the United States and abroad. Although publication implies belief by Potomac Associates in the basic importance and validity of each study, views expressed are those of the authors.

POTOMAC ASSOCIATES is a non-tax-exempt firm, located at 1707 L Street NW, Washington, DC 20036.

A POTOMAC ASSOCIATES BOOK

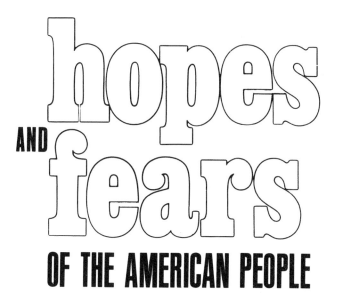

hopes AND fears

OF THE AMERICAN PEOPLE

ALBERT H. CANTRIL and

CHARLES W. ROLL, JR.

Universe Books

NEW YORK

Library of Congress Catalog Card Number: 78-164437
ISBN 0-87663-159-6
Design by Hubert Leckie
Printed in the United States of America

Published in the United States of America in 1971 by Universe Books
381 Park Avenue South, New York, New York 10016
© 1971 by Potomac Associates, Inc.

Contents

Tables

The book in brief

IN JANUARY AND APRIL, 1971, the authors, with the support of Potomac Associates, designed and carried out two public opinion studies. The purpose of this effort was to attain a sense of the basic hopes and fears of the American people and to explore their views on such issues as national unrest and the war in Indochina. Interviews were conducted of representative cross sections of the American population by The Gallup Organization.

The highlights of the findings are:

1. The American people believe their nation is in trouble. They feel that the United States has slid backward over the past five years.

2. Public anxiety over the state of the nation focuses particularly on tensions and divisions among its citizens. Almost one in every two Americans sees these tensions as serious enough to "lead to a real breakdown in this country."

3. The public does not dismiss this national unrest as simply the work of radicals and troublemakers. Sizable numbers sense systemic causes related to the quality of leadership and the performance of institutions.

4. The hopes and fears of the American people about their own lives reflect general satisfaction. There is lessened reference to many traditional material aspirations—a higher standard of living and owning a home, for example—which

11

may indicate overall contentment and assumption of fulfillment of much of the traditional American Dream.

At the same time, there is recognition of a new body of concerns—among them threats to political stability, world peace, and the environment, as well as drugs and crime—demanding social rather than individual solutions.

5. Public opinion toward the Vietnam War has moved dramatically toward disengagement. A clear majority now wants the war ended, even at the risk of an eventual communist takeover of South Vietnam. This sentiment has risen markedly in the last three years and represents a shift since 1968 on the part of one American in four.

6. Public attitude toward existing and future American commitments abroad is one of caution and selectivity. Although the feeling has grown that the nation should concentrate more on domestic than on international problems, it would be an over-simplification to label this mood "isolationism." Rather, the public is critical and discriminating in assessing foreign commitments; its mood appears to range between noninterventionism and selective interventionism.

Preface

NOTHING IS SO ELUSIVE to the analyst of contemporary America as the mood of the people. It is fluid, yet stable. It is inconsistent, yet logical. It both leads and is led.

In our study, we wanted to get beneath the surface of opinion on topical issues. We wanted to examine people's fundamental hopes and fears, which, in the end, contribute to (if not shape) their opinions on specific issues. We aimed at a level of analysis that we believed would be meaningful for those who must make decisions that will determine the quality and direction of American life—a level sufficiently comprehensive to account for the subtleties and contradictions in the mood of America, without being excessively elaborate or cumbersome.

With the support of Potomac Associates, we designed and conducted a public opinion survey through the facilities of The Gallup Organization. A standard sample of 1,588 adult Americans was interviewed between January 8 and 13, 1971. These individuals were selected by established Gallup methods to ensure that they represented a cross section of the nation. The results of this survey proved so intriguing that we prepared a group of subsequent questions that were asked for us of an additional 1,446 respondents by Gallup interviewers between April 2 and 7, 1971.* Our findings comprise this book.

---

* The design and composition of both samples is described in Appendix 2.

We are grateful to all those who helped us, and especially to Dr. Lloyd A. Free, president of the Institute for International Social Research, who generously made the results of his earlier surveys available to us and whose influence upon us both has been most profound.

Albert H. Cantril
Charles W. Roll, Jr.

I

Hopes and fears of the American people

ANALYSTS OF CONTEMPORARY AMERICA make many and varied
assessments of what they see as the unhealthy state of
the nation. The characterizations of the situation differ: a
national crisis of identity, a failure on the part of our major
institutions, the alienation and isolation of the individual.
Central to the concern, no matter how it is expressed, is the
call for a reformulation of old assumptions about how men
relate to each other and to their institutions.

Such a revolution in values ultimately means the abandon-
ment of old assumptions on a scale so broad that new views
will take hold among the public at large. But this is a painful
process, for assumptions will be abandoned only insofar as
frustration with them is truly widespread. The process at
best is uneven, and the resistance is great.

To find out how responsive or resistant Americans are to
such change is what we set out to do. Admittedly, it was an
ambitious undertaking. It involved nothing less than an
attempt to define the basic hopes and fears of the American
people.

To get at this level of opinion, we used a technique that
has become known as the "self-anchoring striving scale."
The technique was developed by the late Hadley Cantril and
his colleague, Lloyd A. Free, in connection with a series of
studies conducted in eighteen different countries between
1958 and 1964 by the Institute for International Social
Research. Their interest was to determine patterns of human

aspiration among people living under varying kinds of political systems and at various stages of national social and economic development.*

In the striving scale technique, the respondent is first asked to describe what life would be like if he were to imagine his future in the "best possible light." This question is open-ended and the respondent's comments are recorded verbatim by the interviewer. The respondent is then asked the opposite: what his future would be like in the "worst possible light." Again, his comments are recorded verbatim. The actual wording of the questions follows:

All of us want certain things out of life. When you think about what really matters in your own life, what are your wishes and hopes for the future? In other words, if you imagine your future in the **best** possible light, what would your life look like then, if you are to be happy? Take your time in answering; such things aren't easy to put into words.

Now, taking the other side of the picture, what are your fears and worries about the future? In other words, if you imagine your future in the **worst** possible light, what would your life look like then? Again, take your time in answering.

The substance of the hopes and fears mentioned is subsequently coded by major categories of concern.

The respondent is next shown a picture of a ladder, symbolic of the ladder of life (see figure 1). The top rung of the ladder, he is told, represents the entire complex of hopes he has just described as the ideal state of affairs, and the bottom

---

* Among countries included in the Institute's studies were the United States, West Germany, Great Britain, France, Japan, Yugoslavia, Poland, Israel, India, the Philippines, Nigeria, Cuba, and the Dominican Republic. The results of the studies appear in: Hadley Cantril, *The Pattern of Human Concerns* (New Brunswick: Rutgers University Press, 1965); Lloyd A. Free and Hadley Cantril, *The Political Beliefs of Americans* (New Brunswick: Rutgers University Press, 1967); and F. P. Kilpatrick and Hadley Cantril, "Self-Anchoring Scaling: A Measure of Individuals' Unique Reality Worlds," *Journal of Individual Psychology*, XVI (November, 1960): 158–73.

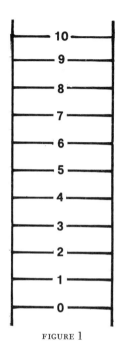

FIGURE 1

rung represents the worst state of affairs. He is then asked to indicate where he feels he stands on the ladder at the present time in relation to his aspirations, where he believes he stood five years ago, and where he thinks he will be five years hence.

The respondent's ladder ratings are self-anchored in that the top and bottom of the ladder are defined in *his own* terms. Thus a present ladder rating of "6" for an upper-middle-class housewife in the New York suburbs is the psychological equivalent of a "6" rating for a sharecropper in the Southwest, even though the substance of their hopes and fears may differ markedly. Further, the respondent's three ladder ratings can be compared, giving a measure of his personal sense of accomplishment (as indicated by the ladder rating shift from past to present) and personal sense of optimism (as indicated by the shift from present to future).

The same series of interrelated questions is then asked about the United States to determine the respondent's hopes and fears for the nation. The respondent is asked to describe the best and worst possible states of affairs for the United States and to indicate national ladder ratings for past, present, and future.

This striving scale has been employed twice before in the United States, in 1959 and 1964, by the Institute for International Social Research. We were able to cite these earlier results, thereby placing our own findings in perspective. In all three surveys, The Gallup Organization was commissioned to do the polling, so there is comparability between the Institute's results and our own.

The American people continue to be preoccupied with two matters—health and their standard of living (see table 1). These two items were cited most frequently as both hopes and fears in 1959, 1964, and 1971, though they were mentioned with considerably less frequency in 1971.

Although the chief hopes and fears expressed by Americans have changed little in the past twelve years, Americans appear to be less preoccupied with what has traditionally comprised the American Dream. This conclusion can be drawn from the decreased frequency with which people mentioned, as either hopes or fears, higher standard of living, fulfillment of aspirations for children, owning a home, availability of leisure time, and assurances of a happy old age.

A change in personal concerns is evident in the topics mentioned more frequently in our January survey than in the earlier studies—drugs, pollution, and crime. These new concerns relate to problems demanding social rather than individual solutions.

One economic matter much on the public's mind is inflation, having bounded into public consciousness over the past few years. In 1959 and 1964, only 1 percent and 3 percent, respectively, spoke of a fear of inflation; in our survey, 11 percent did. Yet concern over unemployment, at a time when the number of people out of work remains high, is not much changed from that of the 1959 and 1964 surveys.

Personal anxiety over international tensions seems to have leveled off. Since 1964, war as a fear has declined, and the slight increase with which peace was mentioned as a personal hope is statistically insignificant. The jump in personal concern over international tensions occurred between 1959 and 1964—years when the cold war was marked by such events as the Cuban missile crisis, the Vienna Summit, and the downing of a U-2 reconnaissance plane over the Soviet Union.

TABLE 1 PERSONAL HOPES AND FEARS
*in percentages**

	personal hopes		
	1959	*1964*	*1971*
Good health for self	40	29	29
Better standard of living	38	40	27
Peace in the world	9	17	19
Achievement of aspirations for children	29	35	17
Happy family life	18	18	14
Good health for family	16	25	13
Own house or live in better one	24	12	11
Peace of mind; emotional maturity	5	9	8
Having wealth	2	5	7
Having leisure time	11	5	6
Happy old age	10	8	6
Good job; congenial work	7	9	6
Employment	5	8	6
Freedom from inflation	1	2	6
Other general concerns for family	7	4	5

	personal fears		
	1959	*1964*	*1971*
Ill health for self	40	25	28
Lower standard of living	23	19	18
War	21	29	17
Ill health for family	25	27	16
Unemployment	10	14	13
Inflation	1	3	11
Unhappy children	12	10	8
Drug problem in family	—·	—	7
Pollution	—	—	7
Political instability	1	2	5
No fears at all	12	10	5
Crime	—	—	5

* A shift of 4 percentage points among the three studies (1959, **1964**, 1971) is considered statistically significant. (For a more detailed explanation, see Appendix 1.)

One of the most important variations in the patterning of concerns is found between the young (those twenty-one to twenty-nine years of age) and their elders. The young people appear to be burgeoning with aspirations. In our January survey, they displayed a greater degree of concern about a broader range of issues than older people did. The young mentioned more frequently concern about a higher standard of living, good family life, a better home, personal wealth, a good job, and solutions to the pollution and crime problems. In only one area were they less concerned than their elders—health. With high hopes, youth has much to be frustrated about and is likely to be impatient.

Table 2 compares the 1959, 1964, and 1971 ladder ratings people gave themselves with respect to their own personal lives. On the whole, these ratings reflect a considerable sense of personal accomplishment: the rating for the present is eight-tenths (+0.8) of a step higher than that for the past— almost a full step on a ten-step ladder. The public is also optimistic about the future: the ladder rating for the future is nine-tenths (+0.9) of a step higher than that for the present. As might be expected, too, young people exhibit the greatest hopefulness in their ladder ratings (see table 3).

Despite the relative satisfaction of Americans at the per-

TABLE 2 PERSONAL LADDER RATINGS

	1959	1964	1971
Rating			
Past	5.9	6.0	5.8
Present	6.6	6.9	6.6
Future	7.8	7.9	7.5
Shift*			
Past to present	+0.7	+0.9	+0.8
Present to future	+1.2	+1.0	+0.9

* A shift of 0.6 in a rating is considered statistically significant.

TABLE 3 PERSONAL LADDER RATING SHIFTS BY
POPULATION GROUPS

	past to present	present to future
	1971	1971
NATIONAL	+0.8	+0.9
Age		
21–29	+1.6	+1.8
30–49	+1.1	+1.2
50 & over	+0.2	+0.1
Education		
College	+1.3	+1.1
High school	+0.9	+1.1
Grade school	0.0	+0.2
Income		
Upper	+1.6	+1.0
Upper middle	+1.1	+1.0
Lower middle	+0.5	+0.8
Lower	−0.1	+0.4
Race		
White	+0.8	+0.9
Nonwhite	+0.4	+1.0

sonal level, significant pockets of frustration and hopeless-
ness do exist. Those with only a grade school education
gave themselves a personal ladder rating for the present that
is exactly the same as their rating for the past. Their ladder
rating for the future was just two-tenths (+0.2) of a step
higher than that for the present.

A similar picture emerges among lower income groups:
their ladder rating shows no real movement from past to
present (−0.1 of a step) and no significant increase from
present to future (+0.4 of a step). The relatively static rating for lower income groups may be attributable in part to
the inclusion of a large proportion of retired persons whose
incomes place them within the lowest quarter of the eco-

nomic scale. On the whole, older people generally displayed only slight shifts in their personal ladder ratings.

Significantly, these pockets of despair are *not* concentrated in the nonwhite community. Table 3 shows that there are no truly meaningful differences in ladder-rating shifts between races. Although nonwhites gave themselves lower ladder ratings than whites, on the key point of movement from past to present to future the races differed little in their perceptions.

Although Americans show some apprehension over a range of emergent social concerns, they appear on the whole to be personally rather satisfied with their lot.

HOPES AND FEARS FOR THE UNITED STATES

When it comes to hopes and fears for the United States, however, the picture is one of considerably less assurance. Table 4 makes clear that issues of war and peace have consistently dominated the aspirations and fears Americans have for their nation. In 1971, though, the percentage mentioning war as a fear dropped to 30, from 64 percent in 1959 and 50 percent in 1964. The percentage citing fear of communism has dropped since 1964, too--from 29 percent to only 12 percent. Further, those mentioning reduction of international tensions as a hope declined from 17 percent in 1959 to 7 percent in 1971. These changes probably indicate that the public is moving away from its earlier perception of a bipolar world preoccupied with the threat of nuclear holocaust. In fact, of the 30 percent mentioning fear of war in our study, only 11 percent referred to nuclear war. Another 7 percent spoke of the Vietnam War, and the remaining 12 percent referred to war in general.

As a national issue, the state of the economy is clearly bothering the American people. Concern over inflation has escalated as both a hope and a fear. Hope for economic sta-

TABLE 4 NATIONAL HOPES AND FEARS

in percentages*

	national hopes		
	1959	1964	1971
Peace	48	51	51
Economic stability; no inflation	12	5	18
Employment	13	15	16
National unity	1	9	15
Law and order	3	4	11
Better standard of living	20	28	11
Solution of pollution problems	—	—	10
Settlement of racial problems	14	15	10
Improved public morality	7	10	8
International cooperation; reduced tensions	17	6	7
Solution of drug problem	—	—	6

	national fears		
	1959	1964	1971
War (esp. nuclear war)	64	50	30
National disunity; political instability	3	8	26
Economic instability; inflation	18	13	17
Communism	12	29	12
Lack of law and order	3	5	11
Pollution	—	—	9
Drugs	—	—	7
Racial tensions	—	9	7
Unemployment	7	6	7
Lack of public morality	4	5	6
Loss of personal freedom	4	5	5

* A shift of 4 percentage points among the three studies (1959, 1964, 1971) is considered statistically significant.

bility jumped from 5 percent in 1964 to 18 percent in 1971 at the same time that its converse, fear of economic instability, moved from 13 percent to 17 percent. But, just as we saw with respect to personal hopes and fears, unemployment has not evoked increased national concern—regardless of the continued urgency of the problem.

Drug use and pollution emerged distinctly as new national concerns in our study. One respondent in ten listed solving pollution problems as a hope for the nation; 6 percent cited solution of the drug problem. On the other side of the scale, drugs and pollution were newly cited fears, just as at the personal level. There was virtually no mention of either in 1959 or 1964.

Our most startling finding, however, was a new and urgent concern over national unity, political stability, and law and order. As a hope for the nation, national unity jumped from 1 percent in 1959 to 15 percent in 1971. In other words, one out of every seven Americans in our study cited national unity as an aspiration. Increased mention of hope for law and order was nearly as pronounced. *And, most striking of all, one American in four (26 percent) listed national disunity or political instability as a fear for the nation—a more than threefold increase over 1964.*

The depth of the concern is apparent in the comments of respondents. A forty-nine-year-old accountant in Vermont told the interviewer, "I fear more riots or even revolution if we don't solve some of our present problems." A twenty-two-year-old mother in Nebraska said, "If people do not learn to live together with what they have, they will be fighting and trying to get more and more while people lose their freedom." A forty-seven-year-old mechanic in Texas commented, "We would be tearing and burning everything up. There would be no regard for the other man. If you wanted something, you'd just take it."

As table 5 shows, fear of national disunity and political instability was expressed by all segments of the population: young and old, well and poorly educated, rich and poor, nonwhites and whites, Democrats and Republicans.

This public anxiety about the state of the nation was dramatically revealed by the ladder ratings citizens gave their

TABLE 5 MENTION OF NATIONAL DISUNITY AND
POLITICAL INSTABILITY AS A NATIONAL FEAR
BY POPULATION GROUPS
in percentages

NATIONAL AVERAGE	26
Age	
21–29	29
30–49	24
50 & over	24
Education	
College	26
High school	23
Grade school	24
Income	
Upper	29
Upper middle	28
Lower middle	25
Lower	20
Political affiliation	
Democrat	27
Republican	24
Independent	25
Race	
White	25
Nonwhite	26

country (see table 6). Looking at the United States in January, 1971, Americans gave a rating (on a ten-rung ladder) of 6.2 for five years past, 5.4 for the present, and 6.2 for five years in the future.

In other words, Americans sense that their country has lost rather than gained ground over the past five years—as evidenced by the drop from past to present in the national ladder rating of nearly a full step.

Looking ahead, people expect the United States in 1976—our bicentennial year—to be merely where it was a full decade

TABLE 6 NATIONAL LADDER RATINGS

	1959	1964	1971
Rating			
Past	6.5	6.1	6.2
Present	6.7	6.5	5.4
Future	7.4	7.7	6.2
Shift*			
Past to present	+0.2	+0.4	−0.8
Present to future	+0.7	+1.2	+0.8

* A shift of 0.6 in a rating is considered statistically significant.

earlier, having barely recovered the reverses of the last half decade.

The importance of the drop in the ladder rating from past to present can scarcely be overstated. In the many studies in which the Institute for International Social Research used the striving scale technique, only once did a present national ladder rating fall below that for the past. This occurred in the Philippines in 1959, at a time when the country appeared to lack strong, dynamic leadership and seemed to many of its people to be standing still.*

This sense of national regression is evident among most population groups (see table 7). In particular, the disparities between population groups at varying education and income levels with respect to personal ladder ratings do not appear

* Historically, shifts in ladder ratings have proven very sensitive indicators of national mood. In Cuba, for example, the Institute conducted a study in mid-1960, after Castro's ascent to power. The national ladder ratings showed that the Cuban public was very excited and optimistic about the revolution. There was a jump from past to present of nearly five steps on the ladder and from present to future of just under two. Clearly, with this amount of internal enthusiasm, there was little reason to believe the Cuban population would join an uprising to oust Castro. This fact was given implicit recognition after the abortive Bay of Pigs invasion by Arthur Schlesinger, Jr., then serving as a special assistant to President John F. Kennedy. In a note of acknowledgement to the Institute, Mr. Schlesinger wrote:"I read with interest

TABLE 7 NATIONAL LADDER RATING SHIFTS BY
POPULATION GROUPS

	past to present	present to future
	1971	1971
NATIONAL	−0.8	+0.8
Age		
21–29	−0.6	+1.0
30–49	−0.8	+0.9
50 & over	−1.0	+0.7
Education		
College	−0.6	+0.9
High school	−0.9	+0.8
Grade school	−0.8	+0.7
Income		
Upper	−0.8	+1.0
Upper middle	−0.9	+0.8
Lower middle	−0.7	+0.9
Lower	−0.8	+0.7
Race		
White	−0.9	+0.8
Nonwhite	+0.6	+0.7

in the national ratings. Similarly, there is little difference between age groups.

Where differing assessments do appear is between races. The national ladder rating given by whites declined nearly a

your Cuban report—and only wish that a copy had come to my attention earlier."

Another case was that of the Dominican Republic. National ladder ratings derived from a 1962 survey showed an intense sense of frustration. Almost half of the population gave the country a zero ladder rating for the past, yielding an average past rating of only 1.7. The present rating was just one step higher. The future rating, however, was over four steps above that of the present. These results prompted Lloyd Free to point to a revolutionary situation in the Dominican Republic almost three years before the 1965 crisis actually occurred. These cases, and others, are described in *The Human Dimension: Experiences in Policy Research*, by Hadley Cantril (Rutgers University Press, New Brunswick, New Jersey, 1967).

TABLE 8 NATIONAL LADDER RATING SHIFTS BY RACE

| | past to present | past to present |
	1959	1971
White	+0.3	−0.9
Nonwhite	−0.3	+0.6

full step (− 0.9) from past to present. In contrast, the rating given by nonwhites rose by more than half a step (+ 0.6), indicating that nonwhites sense measurable accomplishment. This shift is in sharp contrast to the situation in 1959, when exactly the opposite pattern obtained (see table 8). While the progress of recent years has quite obviously not resolved the racial crisis, our findings nevertheless indicate that non-whites believe gains have been made at the national level.

The national ladder ratings also reveal that people of all political persuasions believe the nation has slipped (see table 9). Although Democrats and those disapproving of President Nixon's handling of his job naturally sense the greatest decline, they are not alone. Our findings assume greater significance when they are set against those of the highly partisan year of 1964 (see table 10). Then, the sense of

TABLE 9 NATIONAL LADDER RATING SHIFTS
BY POLITICAL PERSUASION

| | past to present | present to future |
	1971	1971
Political affiliation		
Democrat	−1.0	+0.8
Republican	−0.6	+1.0
Independent	−0.8	+0.7
Nixon job rating		
Approve	−0.6	+0.8
Disapprove	−1.2	+0.9

TABLE 10 SHIFTS IN NATIONAL LADDER RATINGS IN
1964 AND 1971 BY POLITICAL AFFILIATION

	past to present	past to present
	1964	1971
Democrats	+1.1	−1.0
Republicans	−0.8	−0.6
Independents	0.0	−0.8

accomplishment over the preceding five years was great
among the Democratic "ins," but the feeling was not shared
by the Republican "outs." Now, however, even among
Republicans, the sense of decline is pronounced.

We found no single predominant cause behind the drop
in the national ladder rating. The sense that the country has
moved backward over the past five years is shared by all
those who mentioned the principal national fears of war,
national disunity, inflation, lack of law and order, communism, and pollution (see table 11).

The hopes and fears expressed by the American people are
thus full of paradox.

On the personal level, Americans express less concern than
they did five or ten years ago with the material elements that

TABLE 11 NATIONAL LADDER RATING SHIFTS BY
MAJOR NATIONAL FEARS

	past to present
	1971
NATIONAL AVERAGE	−0.8
Those mentioning:	
Communism	−1.3
Lack of law and order	−1.1
National disunity and political instability	−0.9
Economic instability and inflation	−0.9
War	−0.7
Pollution	−0.6

have traditionally comprised the American Dream. Their concerns, too, have broadened to include problems that cannot be solved by the individual alone—drugs, inflation, pollution, and crime. In their personal ladder ratings, they display a considerable sense of achievement and optimism.

On the national level, however, the picture differs. Most striking is the degree, in all segments of the population, to which fear of national disunity is expressed. The mood of the people is vividly shown in the ladder ratings they gave their country—a present rating almost one step below that for the past, and a future rating that merely compensates for the ground lost in the last five years. The American people clearly feel their nation is in trouble.

II

Concern over unrest

THE RESULTS AND IMPLICATIONS of the January, 1971, survey proved so provocative that we decided to probe further into the nature of public concern about national unrest and instability and to try to find out how people would define the underlying causes. In early April, therefore, we prepared a new battery of questions that were asked in our behalf by Gallup interviewers across the nation.

We asked:

There has been a lot of talk in the news recently about unrest in our country and ill-feeling between groups. In general, how concerned are you about this unrest and ill-feeling? Do you think it is likely to lead to a real breakdown in this country or do you think it is likely to blow over soon?

We found that the American people regard the problem of disunity and instability as deeply serious.

Almost one out of every two Americans—47 percent—said they believe that national unrest is serious enough to lead to a "real breakdown"; 38 percent believe it will "blow over."

This anxiety is general and widespread. Groups in which the concern is particularly prevalent include those twenty-one to twenty-nine and thirty to forty-nine years old, middle-income groups, political independents, those with high school and college educations, and those disapproving of Mr. Nixon's handling of the presidency (see table 12).

We also found that people generally do not attribute the unrest simply to the work of agitators and radicals. A large

TABLE 12 SERIOUSNESS OF UNREST
in percentages

	likely to lead to breakdown	likely to blow over soon	don't know
NATIONAL AVERAGE	47	38	15
Age			
21–29	57	30	13
30–49	51	35	14
50 & over	37	45	18
Education			
College	49	34	17
High school	49	39	12
Grade school	38	41	21
Income			
Upper	45	40	15
Upper middle	49	39	12
Lower middle	48	37	15
Lower	41	38	21
Political affiliation			
Democrat	45	37	18
Republican	42	45	13
Independent	53	35	12
Nixon job rating			
Approve	43	44	13
Disapprove	54	33	13

portion of the public senses institutional and systemic causes.

To determine what Americans believed was behind the unrest, we asked respondents to select, from a list of six reasons, one or two that they believed were "mainly responsible for this unrest and ill-feeling." Three reasons focused on participants in protests and demonstrations; the other three related to the adequacy of leadership and institutions.

Five of the six reasons listed were selected by the public

TABLE 13 REASONS SELECTED FOR UNREST AND
ILL-FEELING
in percentages

Our traditional way of doing things is not working and some basic changes are needed if we are to work together.	34
Some young people have gotten out of hand and have no respect for authority.	32
The protests are largely communist inspired.	31
Our leaders in government and business are not trying hard enough to solve the problems we face and people are losing confidence in them.	31
Some Negroes and other minorities are making unreasonable demands.	31
Many of the problems our country faces are so big that we can't agree on how to solve them.	19
Can't say.	7

as about equally responsible for national unrest and ill-feeling. Each of the five was selected by approximately one in three (see table 13). Thirty-four percent said "our traditional way of doing things is not working and some basic changes are needed if we are to work together." Thirty-two percent stated "some young people have gotten out of hand and have no respect for authority." And 31 percent felt that "the protests are largely communist inspired"; "our leaders in government and business are not trying hard enough to solve the problems we face and people are losing confidence in them"; and "some Negroes and other minorities are making unreasonable demands." The only reason of the six selected by a substantially smaller proportion (19 percent) —that "many of the problems our country faces are so big that we can't agree on how to solve them"—questioned the basic American assumption that no challenge is so big that it is insurmountable.

In order to summarize the responses in a more meaningful way, we grouped the reasons into two categories: those dealing with protesters and those dealing with systemic problems. In the first category we combined the percentages of respondents who pointed to (a) "young people have no respect for authority"; (b) "the protests are largely communist inspired"; and (c) "Negroes and other minorities are making unreasonable demands." In the second category we combined the percentages of those who had selected (a) "our traditional way of doing things is not working"; (b) "our leaders are not trying hard enough"; and (c) "many of the problems are so big." The public divided into these categories rather evenly. Thirty-three percent blamed protesters for unrest; 30 percent blamed systemic causes; 30 percent cited a mix between the two categories; and 7 percent had no opinion.

We then reviewed the data to determine which population groups were more likely to subscribe to the reasons related to protesters, and which to the systemic reasons. This was done by computing, for each population group, the difference between the total percentage points given for the first category as opposed to the second.* Table 14 shows population groups more likely to blame demonstrators for unrest; table 15 shows those groups more likely to blame conditions.

---

* Among those with a grade school education, for example, 23 percent selected "our traditional way of doing things is not working," 16 percent selected "many problems are so big," and 28 percent selected "our leaders are not trying hard enough," for a total of 67 percentage points. On the other hand, 34 percent of those with a grade school education selected "minorities are making unreasonable demands," 34 percent selected "the protests are largely communist inspired," and 40 percent selected "young people have no respect for authority," for a total of 108 percentage points. Thus, in this group, the protester-related reasons (108) exceeded the system-related reasons (67) by 41 percentage points.

TABLE 14 POPULATION GROUPS MORE LIKELY TO
BLAME DEMONSTRATORS FOR UNREST

	points by which total for "protester-related" reasons exceeds total for "system-related" reasons
The grade school educated	+41
People in farmer-headed households	+41
Those 50 years of age or over	+40
Republicans	+37
Those approving of the job President Nixon is doing	+34
The high school educated	+25
People in households headed by those not in the labor market (largely retired people)	+25
Residents of municipalities under 50,000	+22

TABLE 15 POPULATION GROUPS MORE LIKELY TO
BLAME CONDITIONS FOR UNREST

	points by which total for "system-related" reasons exceeds total for "protester-related" reasons
The college educated	+53
Nonwhites	+45
Those twenty-one to twenty-nine years of age	+41
Those disapproving of the job President Nixon is doing	+25
People in households headed by professional and business people	+23

More inclined to what we called the "protester-related"
view were the grade school and high school educated, those
living in rural areas, Republicans, and those approving of
President Nixon's performance. Conversely, those tending

TABLE 16 ISSUES PERCEIVED AS CAUSING PROTEST
in percentages

The war in Vietnam	66
Discrimination against minorities and inequality between the races	37
The impatience of young people with the views of older people	24
Lack of trust in most of the individuals in positions of leadership	23
Dissatisfaction with our system of government and the business establishment	20
The danger of nuclear war	6
Can't say	5

toward what we termed the "system-related" perspective were the college educated, those twenty-one to twenty-nine years of age, nonwhites, and those disapproving of President Nixon's performance. Although to a less pronounced degree than the groups listed above, residents of the South and the Midwest were more likely to blame demonstrators than were residents of the East and the West.

To learn what Americans thought was behind the most visible sign of the unrest—protesters—we asked respondents to select from a list of issues the one or two they felt "most of this protest has been about" (see table 16). Not surprisingly, Vietnam was singled out most frequently, being mentioned by two out of three, with discrimination and racial inequality a distant second choice. Almost one American in four, however, sensed a "lack of trust in most of the individuals in positions of leadership" and one in five cited "dissatisfaction with our system of government and the business establishment."

III

Vietnam and future US commitments

AFTER OUR JANUARY SURVEY, when it became clear that Americans were deeply concerned about national unity, we concluded that we could not successfully measure the mood of the nation without examining the issue that appeared to be most intimately intertwined with current unrest—the Vietnam War. We therefore went back to the people in April with a new series of questions about Vietnam and US international commitments in general.

We wanted our questions to spell out the probable consequences of alternative courses in Vietnam. The opinions expressed, we hoped, would then be based upon a recognition of some of the unpleasant contingencies that may lie ahead as the United States disengages from the war in Indochina. Repeating a carefully phrased question asked by Lloyd Free through the Gallup facilities in 1968, we asked:

Suppose the United States were confronted with a choice of only the two alternatives listed on this card, which one would you rather have the United States follow?

A. End the war by accepting the best possible compromise settlement even though it might sooner or later allow the Vietnamese communists to take over control of South Vietnam.

B. Fight on until a settlement can be reached which will insure that the communists do not get control of South Vietnam.

The responses indicated a dramatic shift of opinion. In 1968, 31 percent of those surveyed wanted to end the war; 62 percent wanted to fight on. *In 1971, a substantial majority*

TABLE 17 VIETNAM WAR ALTERNATIVES

	1968 (%)	1971 (%)	Shift (pts)
End war even though communists might take over sooner or later	31	55	+24
Fight on until settlement insuring communists don't take over	62	36	−26
Can't say	7	9	+ 2
Total	100	100	

—55 percent—wanted to end the war, even at the risk of an eventual communist takeover; only 36 percent wanted to fight on (see table 17).

This shift toward disengagement was apparent among all segments of the population, but those twenty-one to twenty-nine years of age, residents of the West, and nonwhites had moved appreciably farther than other groups (see table 18). The proportion of nonwhites opting for withdrawal was particularly high—73 percent. Regionally, the margin in favor of ending the war was especially wide among residents of the East and the West.

As might be expected, our data show that those twenty-one to twenty-nine are now more opposed to continuing the US effort in Vietnam than any other age group. But as recently as 1968, nearly three-fourths (73 percent) of this group favored fighting on in Vietnam to ensure survival of a noncommunist government in Saigon.

On the issue of withdrawal from Vietnam, we found almost no differences in the positions of Democrats, Republicans, or Independents in 1968 or in 1971 (see table 18). With the exception of presidential popularity ratings, opinion polls on the Vietnam War have never revealed significant partisan differences, even on such substantive issues as the bombing of North Vietnam, peace initiatives, and confidence in the South Vietnamese.*

TABLE 18 VIETNAM WAR ALTERNATIVES BY
POPULATION GROUPS

	end war			fight on		
	1968	1971	shift	1968	1971	shift
	(%)	(%)	(pts)	(%)	(%)	(pts)
NATIONAL AVERAGE	31	55	+24	62	36	−26
Sex						
Men	29	52	+23	66	40	−26
Women	34	57	+23	58	33	−25
Education						
College	38	60	+22	58	35	−23
High school	29	52	+23	66	39	−27
Grade school	30	55	+25	57	30	−27
Age						
21–29	23	61	+38	73	35	−38
30–49	32	51	+19	63	40	−23
50 & over	35	55	+20	56	33	−23
Race						
White	31	53	+22	63	38	−25
Nonwhite	41	73	+32	47	13	−34
Political affiliation						
Democrat	31	54	+23	62	36	−26
Republican	32	56	+24	63	39	−24
Independent	31	55	+24	62	34	−28
Region						
East	38	61	+23	54	31	−23
Midwest	30	49	+19	65	41	−24
South	28	51	+23	64	39	−25
West	27	59	+32	70	33	−37

* A detailed study of opinion about the Vietnam War, including an analysis of party positions, can be found in "The American People, Vietnam, and the Presidency," a paper delivered by Albert H. Cantril to the American Political Science Association in Los Angeles, California, in September, 1970.

In the event of significant reverses in South Vietnam, the American people may have some bitter pills to swallow. It would be difficult and unwise at this point to conjecture about public reaction. We did seek to establish, however, whether American citizens would be more likely to perceive a negative outcome in Vietnam as an affront to national honor or as a gain for the communist world. Since we found that the percentage mentioning communism as a national fear had decreased over the past five years, we anticipated that the specter of an American defeat in Vietnam would cause the greater apprehension.

In the April survey, we asked:

Thinking about all that the United States has done over the years to help the South Vietnamese fight the war, suppose that the entire effort failed as the United States continued to withdraw its troops. Which of these things would really bother you the most—that the communists would be expanding their influence by taking over one more country, or that we had been defeated in Vietnam, losing our first war in this century?

Over half of those surveyed—58 percent—replied that they would be more bothered by the possible expansion of communist influence. Only 18 percent expressed more concern about an American defeat. The remainder gave either qualified responses (13 percent) or expressed no opinion (11 percent).

These findings point to a strong residue of anticommunism, at least at the ideological level, among the American people. Yet, as noted earlier, 55 percent of those surveyed indicated that they would be willing to risk a communist takeover in South Vietnam in order to end the fighting.

This seeming contradiction may be explained by the different perceptions Americans have of issues depending on whether the issues are of an ideological or a more concrete and operational nature. American public opinion often operates on two levels simultaneously, and frequently in a rather schizophrenic fashion, a distinction which developed from a study conducted in 1964 by the Institute for International Social Research.* The study showed that the American public generally demonstrates basic conservatism when confronted with an ideological issue but, at the same time, responds more liberally when confronted with an operational issue. A similar pattern seems to appear in relation to the Vietnam War, the public being pretty tough-minded at the ideological level but more concerned with concrete gains at the operational level.

There has been speculation that, as a result of the Vietnam War, we are turning inward as a nation, seeking a kind of "normalcy" as we did in the aftermath of World War I and the Paris Peace Conference. Our data, however, show a more complicated picture.

To determine whether the US population believed its government should give precedence to domestic or international problems, we asked whether respondents agreed or

---

* In the study, the Institute asked Americans whether they agreed or disagreed with a number of propositions about the general role of the federal government in the solution of domestic problems. One battery of questions was couched in essentially ideological terms, such as "the federal government is interfering too much in state and local matters"; "we should rely more on individual initiative and ability and not so much on governmental welfare programs." The other battery of questions referred to specific federal programs: "a broad general program of federal aid to education," "a compulsory medical insurance program covering hospital and nursing care for the elderly," and so on.

At the ideological level, the public was predominantly "conservative," opposed to an extensive role for the federal government in domestic affairs. At the operational level, however, the public was overwhelmingly "liberal," supportive of an active federal government role. The study concluded: "While the old argument about the 'welfare state' has long since been resolved at the operational level of government programs, it most definitely *has not* been resolved at the ideological level." (Lloyd A. Free and Hadley Cantril, *The Political Beliefs of Americans*, New Brunswick: Rutgers University Press, 1967, p. 40.)

TABLE 19 PERCENTAGE OF AGREEMENT AND
DISAGREEMENT WITH CONCENTRATING
MORE ON DOMESTIC PROBLEMS

	1964	1968	1971
Agree	55	60	77
Disagree	32	31	16
No opinion	13	9	7

disagreed with this statement: "We shouldn't think so much in **international** terms but concentrate more on our own **national** problems and building up our strength and prosperity here at home."

Over three-fourths of the public—77 percent—agreed. Only 16 percent disagreed. The same question was asked in 1964 and 1968 by the Institute for International Social Research and, as table 19 shows, there has been considerable shift on this issue over the last three years. In 1964, 55 percent agreed and 32 percent disagreed; in 1968, the respective percentages were 60 and 31. This impressive shift, furthermore, has occurred about equally among all population groups (see table 20).

There are significant differences, however, in the extent to which various population groups favor concentrating on domestic problems. In general, our findings show that the higher the education and income level, the greater the probability of an internationalist stance.

This shift in opinion toward emphasis on domestic issues does not appear to be accompanied by a sanguine view that real world peace is closer than it has been in the past. When asked whether the "chances of a major world war breaking out have increased or decreased in recent years," 46 percent of those surveyed—almost one in two—said the likelihood of a major war had increased. Only one in three (33 percent) saw a lessening of the threat of war. Twelve percent believed

TABLE 20 PERCENTAGE FAVORING CONCENTRATION
ON DOMESTIC PROBLEMS BY
POPULATION GROUPS

	1968 (%)	1971 (%)	shift (pts)
NATIONAL AVERAGE	60	77	+17
Sex			
Men	62	76	+14
Women	57	79	+22
Education			
College	51	66	+15
High school	59	79	+20
Grade school	71	85	+14
Age			
21–29	59	79	+20
30–49	56	73	+17
50 & over	64	81	+17
Race			
White	58	77	+19
Nonwhite	73	84	+11
Political affiliation			
Democrat	58	80	+22
Republican	61	75	+14
Independent	60	77	+17

there had been no appreciable change, and 9 percent
expressed no opinion. Again, variations in educational and
income levels accounted for significant differences. The college educated and the economically well-off were more likely
to believe chances of war had decreased.

To ascertain what lay behind belief that the chances of
war had increased or decreased, we asked each respondent to
select from a list of eight reasons the one or two he thought
made it more (or less) likely that a major war would break
out.

Those who believe that chances of major war have

TABLE 21 REASONS SELECTED FOR BELIEF A
MAJOR WAR IS MORE LIKELY
*(Asked only of those saying chances of a major war have
increased in recent years)*
in percentages

Even though people may be tired of war and want peace, there will always be sources of conflict that the major powers will not be able to keep from turning into larger wars.	15
Communist China is still working hard to cause trouble in Asia and will try to spread its influence throughout the world regardless of the cost in human lives.	15
The Russians have always been aggressive and they will always try to expand their influence.	13
The difficulties the United States has had in Vietnam will encourage the communists to cause trouble elsewhere in the world.	12
Regardless of what people say, Russia and China are allies and will continue to work together, especially when the going gets tough.	8
The poor and backward nations of the world are so weak that there is always the chance that some local conflict will be blown up into a world problem.	7
The United States has cut back on its military defenses and is not as able to deal with any threat as it was.	5
Can't say.	2
None of these reasons (volunteered).	1

increased cited four principal reasons: there will always be
sources of conflict (selected by 15 percent), Communist
China will always want to cause trouble (15 percent)*, the
Soviet Union is basically aggressive (13 percent), and US
difficulties in Vietnam will promote communist adventurism

* This sampling was taken prior to the visit of a US table tennis team to
Communist China. Accordingly, the data do not reflect any impact this
event may have had on public opinion.

elsewhere (12 percent). (See table 21.) The traditional argument that cutting back on US defenses will embolden the country's adversaries did not draw much support (5 percent)—even among those who felt that chances of major war had increased.

The principal reasons cited by those who believe chances of war have decreased were: people everywhere are simply tired of war (selected by 14 percent), the Soviet Union has become more interested in world peace (12 percent), and the difficulties experienced by the United States in Vietnam will discourage hasty American involvement in the future (11 percent). (See table 22.)

In addition, we wanted to know how willing the American people would be to come to the aid of countries under attack by communist-backed forces—a question that carries immense implications for policy. We asked:

In the event a nation is attacked by communist-backed forces, there are several things the United States can do about it. As I read the name of each country, tell me what action you would want to see us take if that nation is actually attacked—send American troops **or** send military supplies but not send American troops **or** refuse to get involved at all?

Each respondent was then read the names of eleven countries. The pattern of responses, shown in table 23, was mixed. *In no case, however, did a majority favor sending US troops to the aid of any of the countries listed—including two of our NATO allies, England and West Germany.*

Except for Yugoslavia, presumably regarded by many as just another communist power, the willingness of the public to aid in the defense of a country varied almost directly with the proximity of that country to the United States. Mexico and England received the lowest "refuse to get involved" response (19 percent), followed by West Germany (22 percent), Brazil and Israel (33 percent), Turkey

TABLE 22 REASONS SELECTED FOR BELIEF A
MAJOR WAR IS LESS LIKELY
*(Asked only of those saying chances of a major war have
decreased in recent years)*
in percentages

People everywhere are tired of war and there are new kinds of international cooperation that are becoming more and more important.	14
The Russians now feel that it is in their own interest to be more cooperative and work for world peace.	12
America has learned a lesson from Vietnam and will not be so quick to become involved in similar situations in the future.	11
The United States is strong enough to keep other nations from risking war.	9
The Russians and the Chinese are no longer working together and are not the combined threat they used to be.	7
The poor and backward nations of the world are making enough progress so that there are fewer reasons for local conflicts to be blown up into world problems.	2
Communist China has been so busy dealing with its own internal problems that it has become less aggressive.	2
None of these reasons (volunteered).	1
Can't say.	1

(37 percent), Japan and Thailand (38 percent), India (39 percent), Nationalist China (45 percent), and Yugoslavia (51 percent). Sending American troops even to the defense of such nations as West Germany, England, and Japan, the integrity of which has been of vital strategic interest to the United States, does not marshal much enthusiasm, supported by only 37 percent, 28 percent, and 17 percent, respectively.

In general, however, large numbers of Americans support sending supplies to a country under attack by communist-

TABLE 23 US RESPONSE IN EVENT A NATION IS
ATTACKED BY COMMUNIST-BACKED FORCES

in percentages

	should send troops	should send supplies only	should refuse to get involved	can't say
Mexico	45	26	19	10
England	37	33	19	11
West Germany	28	41	22	9
Brazil	16	36	33	15
Israel	11	44	33	12
Turkey	10	36	37	17
Japan	17	34	38	11
Thailand	11	36	38	15
India	7	40	39	14
Nationalist China	11	30	45	14
Yugoslavia	7	27	51	15

backed forces, a finding that suggests considerable public backing for the Nixon Doctrine and even for a broadening of its terms.

The Nixon Doctrine does not preclude American military intervention in the event of communist-supported armed attack against an American ally or another nation considered vital to our security. Instead, it promises to limit the American response to military and economic assistance in cases involving aggression short of overt armed attack. Our data indicate, however, that large numbers of the public would prefer to keep the American response limited to military assistance, short of sending troops, even if our allies were directly attacked by communist-backed forces.

It should be noted that the definition of this middle position in our question specifically stated "send military supplies but not send American troops." The group favoring this position represents a very large segment of responses for many countries on the list. In the face of an actual crisis—with communist troops massing on the border of a threatened country, reports of increased insurgent activity, or imminent collapse of a regime friendly to the United States, all occurring after US military aid had been provided —this group of respondents would face a difficult choice. Would these people then simply say enough, no more? Or would they shift toward support for sending American troops? Much, of course, would depend on which country was threatened, as well as on how American leadership positioned the issue for the public. No doubt, in some cases, support for direct intervention with US forces would grow substantially.

The case of Nationalist China deserves particular mention. Only 11 percent of those surveyed believed troops should be sent in the event of a communist-backed attack; only 30 percent more would support sending military supplies. Forty-five percent said they believed the United States should do nothing. At the present, the public appears to be less concerned about the fate of the Chiang Kai-shek government on Taiwan than many political leaders have long assumed.

To determine who would be most reluctant to see the United States become involved internationally in the defense of a nation under attack, we averaged, for all eleven countries, the refuse-to-get-involved responses by population groups.* We found that those twenty-one to twenty-nine, the middle-aged, those with college educations, and those in upper income groups were the least reluctant to come to the aid of other nations (see table 24). As in the case of the shift of opinion toward disengagement in Vietnam, there were no discernible partisan differences. But, unlike opinion on

---

* For example, among twenty-one to twenty-nine year olds, 14 percent said that the United States should refuse to get involved in Mexico, 15 percent with respect to England, 18 percent for West Germany, 27 percent for Brazil, etc., yielding an eleven-country "reluctance" average of 29 percent for the youngest age group.

TABLE 24 OPPOSITION TO INTERVENTION BY
POPULATION GROUPS

	11-country average of refuse-to-get-involved responses (%)	points between highest and lowest refuse-to-get-involved responses
Education		
College	29	41
High school	33	33
Grade school	40	22
Age		
21–29	29	36
30–49	30	34
50 & over	40	28
Income		
Upper	29	39
Upper middle	31	36
Lower middle	33	33
Lower	42	20
Political affiliation		
Democrat	34	26
Republican	34	35
Independent	32	37

Vietnam, there were virtually no regional differences, either.
Yet those most willing to assist foreign nations (the young, the middle-aged, the well educated, the economically better off) were also most selective in choosing countries to which the United States should give military aid. As a rough measure of selectivity for each population group, we used the range of percentage points between the country with the highest refuse-to-get-involved response and the country with the lowest refuse-to-get-involved response (see second column of table 24).*

* For example, among twenty-one to twenty-nine-year olds, the highest refuse-to-get-involved response was 50 percent for Yugoslavia, and the lowest, 14 percent for Mexico, for a "selectivity" range of 36 percentage points.

Were an actual crisis upon us, the public would probably be more supportive of involvement—even to the extent of committing US forces—than these data suggest. Nonetheless, it seems fair to say that the American people show caution and reserve in regard to foreign military interventions. Whether this mood can be defined as "isolationism" is dubious. It appears to be marked instead by considerable ambivalence and discrimination, and to range from noninterventionism to selective interventionism.

IV

A troubled nation

THE NATIONAL MOOD IS ONE OF SEEMING PARADOX: grave apprehension about the state of the nation juxtaposed against a tempered sense of personal achievement and optimism.

The American people are clearly troubled about the state of their country. Traditional optimism about the nation's steady progress has faltered. The average American feels that the United States has slid backward over the past five years. Major contributors to this widespread and pervasive mood of disquiet include increased awareness of national divisions, anxiety about the breakdown in law and order, diminished but nevertheless still important concern about the threat of war, growing opposition to the war in Indochina, and uncertainty over the economy.

Nearly half of the American population believes that current unrest is so serious that "a real breakdown in this country" may be in the offing. The unrest is not dismissed as solely the work of radicals or troublemakers. Americans see systemic causes, too: failure of our traditional way of doing things and inadequacy of national leadership—both within government and without. Many agree there is need for basic changes before confidence can be restored.

Yet, despite deep public apprehension over the state of the nation, the American people display a sense of accomplishment in terms of their personal aspirations and look forward to continuing progress in the years ahead. And at present they can view this personal satisfaction quite apart from their concerns for the nation as a whole.

Americans now appear less preoccupied with attainment of many basic material goals that once were central to their aspirations and comprised much of the traditional American Dream. At the same time, these personal hopes and fears, predominantly of a "bread and butter" nature, seem to be yielding to another set of concerns, which reflect emergent social and political problems that are increasingly forcing their way into people's lives: inflation, drugs, pollution, crime, and political instability.

Although people are apprehensive about what they see going on around them, they cannot be characterized as distressed, confused, or groping when it comes to their individual lives. The new genre of concerns at the personal level has not, in our view, created the deep frustrations that might produce the revolution in values heralded by some critics of contemporary America. The topics at issue have not, as yet, impinged sufficiently upon the individual's daily routine and well-being to preclude his enjoyment of the good life.

This judgment should not, however, inspire any false sense of confidence. Our data clearly show urgent and rapidly rising public concern about national unrest and leadership. And the possibility certainly exists that at some future point the public may make a direct linkage between their personal and national hopes and fears. Implicit in this, of course, is a resultant intensification of public concern at both levels.

Other factors may contribute to a more charged atmosphere. The public faces continuing frustration and anxiety, bombarded as it is in our information-saturated society with details of problems at home and abroad about which the individual can do little. There is even a danger that this seemingly constant succession of national and international problems of crisis proportions may drive the public to a point beyond which mobilization for any cause, no matter how meritorious or pressing, will be increasingly difficult.

At a time when the public's confidence has been so shaken, the quality of leadership ahead is crucial. Given the urgency of public anxiety over the nation's health, we believe the American people are particularly susceptible to a full range of initiatives that could be put before them:

• The opportunity for the demagogue is great. An appeal can easily be mounted that would exploit deep-rooted fears of national disunity and lack of law and order at home or would oversimplify our role in world affairs.

• An alternative course is to try to calm a troubled nation with uncritical reassertions of the legitimacy of our traditions, symbols, and institutions. Such an appeal would stress maintenance of the *status quo*. It would aim to satisfy public desire to protect gains already made, rather than venture beyond these gains to a new level of public commitment and participation in national and international problem-solving.

• Or—taking an affirmative course—national leadership can respond to and build upon the public's growing awareness and understanding of our pressing problems. Leadership both in and out of government—regardless of political persuasion or affiliation—can move ahead of the people and take as its keynote the public's sense that new priorities and approaches are needed.

Above all, a nation whose spirit is so troubled needs hope. Rhetoric alone will not suffice. The hope must be real, grounded in a national awareness and understanding of emerging trends that make clear we can begin to pull together to solve our problems. When affirmative courses and actions are presented by our national leaders, and when they keep the public forthrightly informed about difficulties expected in tackling the jobs ahead, we believe the public will go a long way toward accepting fundamentally new approaches and making the required sacrifices.

Appendix 1 Tables, with a guide for their interpretation

THE DATA DERIVED IN OUR SURVEYS in January and April, 1971, have dimensions of interest that extend in many respects beyond the conclusions highlighted in this brief book. For those interested, we have included in this appendix relatively complete tables of results for all the questions we asked.

A word of introduction is needed, however, for the reader without prior experience in statistical analysis. Conclusions should be drawn from our data only with a sense of the inherent complexity of opinion polling and the inevitable margin of sampling error to which all such surveys are subject.

Sampling error, in simplest terms, means the extent to which results obtained in a survey may differ from those that would be derived if the whole population had been interviewed, rather than only a representative sample. The size of a sampling error depends largely on the number of interviews conducted. This type of error has been taken into account in all conclusions drawn in the text of this book.

There are two kinds of margin of sampling errors which are useful to have in mind when interpreting the reported data.

SAMPLING ERROR OF A PERCENTAGE

A margin of error must be allowed for each percentage. This margin indicates the range (plus or minus a specified number

We are indebted to Paul K. Perry, president of The Gallup Organization, for his assistance in preparing this guide.

of percentage points) within which the results of repeated samplings in the same time period could have been expected to vary, 95 percent of the time, assuming the same sampling procedure, the same interviewers, and the same questionnaire.

Table A shows how much allowance should be made for percentages relating to the sample as a whole and for those relating to a portion of the total sample.

For the sample as a whole (about 1,500 cases), table A is to be used in the following manner: Let us say a reported percentage is 33 and the total number of persons interviewed is 1,500. In the row headed "percentages near 30" on the left side of the table, go across to the column headed "1,500." The number there is "3," which means that the 33 percent obtained in the sample is subject to a sampling error of plus or minus 3 points. In other words, very probably (ninety-five chances out of one hundred) the average of repeated samplings would be somewhere between thirty and thirty-six, with the most likely figure being the thirty-three obtained.

For a portion of the total sample (such as those with a college education), look first at table A-17 on page 92, which shows the composition of the samples. The table indicates that in our surveys there were about four hundred college educated persons interviewed (447 in the January study and 401 in the April study). Again, taking a reported percentage of 33, follow the row "percentages near 30" across to the column headed "400." The number there is "6," indicating that the margin to be allowed for sampling error for college educated persons is plus or minus 6 points.

SAMPLING ERROR OF A DIFFERENCE BETWEEN PERCENTAGES

In comparing two percentages, the question arises as to how large the difference between them must be before one can be reasonably sure it reflects a real difference. The number

TABLE A RECOMMENDED ALLOWANCE FOR SAMPLING
ERROR OF A PERCENTAGE

In Percentage Points (at 95 in 100 confidence level)*

			Size of the Sample				
	1500	1000	750	600	400	200	100
Percentages near 10	2	2	3	3	4	5	7
Percentages near 20	2	3	4	4	5	7	9
Percentages near 30	3	4	4	4	6	8	10
Percentages near 40	3	4	4	5	6	8	11
Percentages near 50	3	4	4	5	6	8	11
Percentages near 60	3	4	4	5	6	8	11
Percentages near 70	3	4	4	4	6	8	10
Percentages near 80	2	3	4	4	5	7	9
Percentages near 90	2	2	3	3	4	5	7

* The chances are 95 in 100 that the sampling error is not larger than the figures shown.

of points which must be allowed for in such comparisons is indicated in table B. The upper half of table B should be used for percentages near 20 or 80; the lower half for percentages near 50. For percentages in between, the error to be allowed for is between those shown in the table.

When comparing the difference in percentages between two separate surveys (1964 and 1971, for example), the table should be used as follows. Let us say 50 percent in 1964 and 40 percent in 1971 responded in a certain way to the same question, yielding a difference of ten percentage points between the two studies. Since the percentages are near 50, and both studies were based on samples of about 1,500 cases each, consult the lower half of table B under the column headed "1,500" in the row designated "1,500." The number there is "5." This means that the allowance for error is 5 points. The percentage for 1964 is therefore somewhere between 5 and 15 points higher than the percentage for 1971. In other words, we can conclude with considerable confidence that a difference exists in the direction observed and that it amounts to

TABLE B **RECOMMENDED ALLOWANCE FOR SAMPLING ERROR OF A DIFFERENCE BETWEEN PERCENTAGES**

In Percentage Points (at 95 in 100 confidence level)*

Size of the Sample	Percentages near 20 or percentages near 80				
	1500	750	600	400	200
1500	4				
750	4	5			
600	5	5	6		
400	6	6	6	7	
200	8	8	8	8	10

Size of the Sample	Percentages near 50				
	1500	750	600	400	200
1500	5				
750	5	6			
600	6	7	7		
400	7	7	8	8	
200	10	10	10	10	12

* The chances are 95 in 100 that the sampling error is not larger than the figures shown.

no less than 5 percentage points. If, in another case, 1964 responses amounted to 22 percent, and 1971 responses to 24 percent, you would have to consult the top portion of table B since these percentages are near 20. Assuming a sample of 1,500 cases in each survey, the margin of sampling error is "4." In this case, the 2-point difference is inconclusive.

When comparing the difference in percentages within one study, first consult table A-17 to determine the number of cases involved, and then proceed as above.

TABLE A-1 PERSONAL HOPES, 1971 by percent

	good health for self	better living standard	peace, no wars	aspirations for children	happy family life	good family health	own house or better one
NATIONAL	29	27	19	17	14	13	11
Sex							
Men	28	30	15	11	14	8	9
Women	30	24	24	21	14	18	13
Race							
White	29	27	20	16	14	14	10
Nonwhite	29	27	9	22	9	4	20
Education							
College	17	28	19	18	20	15	8
High school	29	29	20	19	14	13	12
Grade school	40	23	19	10	9	12	11
Occupation							
Prof. & bus.	22	28	21	20	17	17	8
White collar	25	34	17	24	18	13	11
Farmers	32	26	25	19	14	8	8
Manual	25	29	18	18	16	14	13
Nonlabor force	46	18	21	4	5	10	10
Age							
21–29 years	12	32	14	18	29	14	22
30–49 years	24	28	19	27	12	16	9
50 & over	41	23	22	8	8	11	7
Politics							
Republican	28	26	18	16	16	16	9
Democrat	31	25	20	17	12	11	12
Independent	26	31	20	16	16	13	12
Region							
East	32	29	19	15	16	15	12
Midwest	33	24	22	19	14	14	10
South	27	29	17	18	13	13	13
West	19	26	21	12	12	10	8
Income							
$15,000 & over	22	29	23	27	17	23	5
$7,000–$14,999	26	28	20	19	15	13	10
$5,000–$6,999	30	27	13	12	18	9	15
Under $5,000	37	24	21	10	8	10	13
Community Size							
Over 500,000	29	26	20	15	14	13	10
50,000–499,999	26	29	21	18	15	12	13
2,500–49,999	30	30	16	20	15	10	10
Under 2,500	29	26	19	16	13	16	11

peace of mind	wealth	recreation, travel, leisure time	good job, congenial work	happy old age	economic stability in general	employ-ment	concern for family, relatives
8	7	6	6	6	6	6	5
7	9	6	8	7	7	7	4
9	5	6	4	5	4	5	6
8	7	6	5	6	6	6	5
9	6	3	14	6	4	5	7
8	7	9	7	6	6	5	6
8	8	5	7	6	5	6	4
8	5	5	3	6	8	5	6
9	7	5	4	4	5	6	5
7	7	6	5	4	7	6	5
12	8	5	—	5	6	4	7
6	8	6	9	8	7	8	5
8	3	7	3	6	4	1	5
6	11	5	11	2	4	4	7
8	8	7	7	5	5	9	5
9	4	6	2	9	7	4	4
7	5	4	5	5	6	5	5
6	6	6	6	8	7	6	5
10	9	9	7	4	3	6	5
9	7	8	6	8	4	7	4
8	9	5	5	7	5	6	4
8	6	4	7	4	4	5	8
4	4	7	7	5	10	5	4
8	6	8	3	8	4	8	3
6	9	7	7	6	7	6	5
9	6	7	6	4	6	6	3
10	4	3	6	6	4	3	8
9	8	7	6	7	5	5	4
6	7	7	8	7	7	6	6
7	5	6	4	6	5	5	3
9	6	5	5	4	6	6	7

TABLE A-2 PERSONAL FEARS, 1971 by percent

	poor health for self	worse living standard	war	poor health for family	unemployment	econom instabi
NATIONAL	26	18	17	16	13	11
Sex						
Men	28	17	14	13	16	14
Women	23	18	19	19	10	9
Race						
White	26	17	17	17	12	12
Nonwhite	26	29	6	8	21	6
Education						
College	24	16	16	17	12	12
High school	25	20	17	20	15	11
Grade school	29	15	16	8	9	10
Occupation						
Prof. & bus.	25	19	16	21	15	13
White collar	23	19	18	13	13	11
Farmers	29	22	8	13	6	14
Manual	25	19	18	18	16	11
Nonlabor force	30	13	15	10	6	9
Age						
21–29 years	19	20	19	22	19	11
30–49 years	25	19	17	20	16	9
50 & over	30	15	15	10	6	13
Politics						
Republican	26	17	15	18	12	11
Democrat	26	18	15	16	11	12
Independent	25	18	21	15	16	11
Region						
East	26	15	18	19	10	10
Midwest	27	18	16	16	14	11
South	26	18	16	15	12	10
West	23	20	16	12	16	15
Income						
$15,000 & over	26	19	17	20	15	15
$7,000–$14,999	25	16	18	20	15	10
$5,000–$6,999	27	20	16	14	13	13
Under $5,000	26	20	14	9	9	9
Community Size						
Over 500,000	26	19	17	17	15	9
50,000–499,999	29	17	17	18	15	10
2,500–49,999	22	18	14	11	12	12
Under 2,500	25	16	17	16	9	13

children unsuccessful or unhappy	drugs	pollution	political instability	no fears	crime
8	7	7	5	5	5
4	4	7	5	6	4
11	10	7	5	4	5
7	7	7	5	5	4
14	4	1	4	7	10
5	6	11	7	3	4
10	8	7	5	4	4
6	7	4	4	7	7
8	8	11	8	3	4
11	9	6	4	3	5
3	4	4	5	4	3
10	9	6	4	5	5
3	3	4	4	9	6
10	5	9	6	3	2
12	12	7	6	3	4
4	4	6	4	7	6
7	7	6	5	7	6
8	7	7	5	5	5
8	6	8	6	3	3
10	9	9	4	5	6
7	7	6	4	6	5
9	7	4	6	4	4
3	4	9	6	3	3
8	7	11	8	3	3
9	8	8	6	4	5
8	7	4	3	6	6
6	6	4	3	7	5
6	6	8	4	4	7
6	8	8	6	5	3
9	7	7	6	5	3
10	8	5	4	6	3

TABLE A-3 HOPES FOR NATION, 1971 by percent

	peace, no wars	economic stability	enough employment	national unity	law & order
NATIONAL	51	18	16	15	11
Sex					
Men	47	19	15	15	11
Women	55	17	16	14	10
Race					
White	52	19	15	15	11
Nonwhite	41	6	17	14	10
Education					
College	44	20	15	17	7
High school	54	20	16	15	11
Grade school	52	11	15	12	13
Occupation					
Prof. & bus.	46	23	16	16	7
White collar	49	19	11	15	11
Farmers	52	18	9	11	12
Manual	53	17	21	14	12
Nonlabor force	54	13	10	16	12
Age					
21–29 years	51	23	14	17	9
30–49 years	54	18	21	15	11
50 & over	49	15	12	13	11
Politics					
Republican	52	20	17	17	9
Democrat	51	17	15	13	10
Independent	51	16	15	16	13
Region					
East	55	17	15	14	7
Midwest	54	19	17	13	14
South	49	16	13	17	10
West	43	19	19	16	12
Income					
$15,000 & over	47	20	19	19	8
$7,000–$14,999	51	19	17	14	10
$5,000–$6,999	52	20	13	11	12
Under $5,000	54	13	13	15	12
Community Size					
Over 500,000	50	16	20	14	9
50,000–499,999	49	24	14	17	11
2,500–49,999	51	18	13	13	12
Under 2,500	55	15	13	15	11
Nixon Job Rating					
Approve	51	18	16	16	11
Disapprove	51	18	16	12	9

better living standard	solution of pollution problems	settlement of racial problems, social justice	public morality and ethics	internat'l co-op, reduced tensions	solution of drug problem
11	10	10	8	8	6
11	8	8	6	8	5
11	12	13	9	8	7
11	11	10	8	8	6
10	2	12	3	5	7
12	17	16	8	10	4
11	8	10	8	7	6
10	7	7	7	7	7
13	17	15	9	8	4
11	9	13	6	8	7
9	5	7	9	7	10
11	10	10	6	8	7
9	6	6	11	8	5
12	17	17	5	11	5
11	10	10	8	6	9
11	6	8	9	7	5
14	10	8	8	7	6
11	9	11	6	9	6
9	11	13	10	6	5
14	9	12	5	10	6
13	10	13	10	7	7
6	7	7	8	8	6
12	16	7	10	4	5
14	20	15	8	13	5
12	10	11	7	7	7
10	7	9	7	7	4
12	6	7	9	6	7
14	10	12	6	9	5
9	10	13	9	7	7
9	11	11	9	7	3
11	10	6	7	7	8
9	9	6	8	8	6
9	12	8	5	7	6

TABLE A-4 FEARS FOR NATION, 1971 by percent

	war	political instability, national disunity	economic instability	communism	lack of law & order
NATIONAL	30	26	17	12	11
Sex					
Men	30	26	17	13	11
Women	31	23	17	12	11
Race					
White	31	25	18	13	11
Nonwhite	24	26	9	4	15
Education					
College	28	31	18	16	8
High school	31	23	18	13	11
Grade school	31	24	12	7	15
Occupation					
Prof. & bus.	33	30	18	15	10
White collar	26	26	20	22	7
Farmers	25	27	16	14	10
Manual	31	24	16	11	13
Nonlabor force	31	23	15	6	12
Age					
21–29 years	34	29	16	11	8
30–49 years	30	24	17	15	13
50 & over	28	24	17	11	11
Politics					
Republican	30	24	17	16	12
Democrat	30	27	17	10	12
Independent	30	25	17	12	11
Region					
East	36	22	15	8	8
Midwest	28	25	17	14	12
South	27	28	15	14	15
West	30	25	21	15	10
Income					
$15,000 & over	30	29	20	16	9
$7,000–$14,999	30	28	18	12	11
$5,000–$6,999	32	25	14	15	13
Under $5,000	30	20	15	8	12
Community Size					
Over 500,000	33	23	15	9	12
50,000–499,999	27	33	18	14	9
2,500–49,999	31	23	18	17	10
Under 2,500	29	25	18	12	13
Nixon Job Rating					
Approve	29	25	16	14	10
Disapprove	34	25	19	11	12

pollution	drugs	racial tensions	unemployment	lack of public morality	lack or loss of freedom
9	7	7	7	6	5
8	5	7	5	4	4
9	9	7	8	7	5
9	7	7	7	6	5
1	9	6	7	3	—
14	4	7	5	7	7
8	8	8	8	6	4
4	9	4	6	4	3
16	5	11	6	5	7
10	4	8	5	12	3
2	9	5	3	4	5
7	10	6	8	5	4
5	6	5	6	4	4
13	7	7	8	4	6
10	10	8	6	7	6
5	5	6	6	5	3
8	9	5	4	6	6
7	6	7	7	5	3
11	6	9	9	6	6
12	5	8	7	4	4
7	9	9	7	7	7
5	8	6	5	7	3
12	5	3	8	4	4
14	7	9	7	10	7
10	7	7	6	5	5
6	5	6	6	5	5
5	9	6	7	4	2
11	4	7	8	4	5
9	10	6	5	8	5
6	5	8	7	7	4
7	9	7	5	5	4
9	8	7	6	6	5
9	5	8	8	6	5

TABLE A-5 PERSONAL LADDER RATINGS BY DEMOGRAPHIC GROUPS

	Past		Present		Future	
	1964	1971	1964	1971	1964	1971
NATIONAL	5.96	5.75	6.85	6.56	7.89	7.50
Sex						
Men	5.89	5.61	6.76	6.40	7.74	7.33
Women	6.02	5.92	6.92	6.62	8.03	7.65
Race						
White	6.06	5.79	6.96	6.63	7.92	7.54
Nonwhite	5.11	5.34	5.84	5.77	7.72	6.75
Education						
College	6.29	5.69	7.26	7.03	8.24	8.14
High school	5.79	5.58	6.76	6.46	7.96	7.57
Grade school	6.03	6.24	6.73	6.28	7.53	6.54
Occupation						
Prof. & bus.	6.19	5.87	7.26	7.18	8.14	8.23
White collar	5.82	5.66	7.03	6.49	8.26	7.51
Farmers	6.09	5.82	6.78	6.12	7.51	7.30
Manual	5.46	5.36	6.61	6.33	8.00	7.58
Nonlabor force	7.06	6.61	6.88	6.50	7.04	7.03
Age						
21–29 years	5.08	4.66	6.39	6.26	8.34	8.07
30–49 years	5.58	5.55	6.82	6.62	8.14	7.84
50 & over	6.72	6.49	7.04	6.66	7.33	6.80
Politics						
Republican	6.37	6.19	7.20	6.77	7.83	7.58
Democrat	5.81	5.80	6.67	6.47	7.90	7.32
Independent	5.86	5.23	6.88	6.43	7.96	7.68
Region						
East	5.87	5.77	6.92	6.63	7.96	7.60
Midwest	6.07	5.83	6.95	6.56	7.97	7.44
South	6.00	5.58	6.70	6.48	7.78	7.28
West	5.65	5.95	6.78	6.52	7.85	7.67
Income						
Upper	6.12	5.90	7.41	7.49	8.47	8.50
Upper middle	5.83	5.64	7.03	6.76	8.07	7.76
Lower middle	5.72	5.95	6.52	6.48	7.62	7.30
Lower	6.23	6.04	6.27	5.93	7.06	6.32
Community Size						
500,000 & over	5.76	5.72	6.65	6.56	7.06	6.32
50,000–499,999	5.83	5.96	6.82	6.59	8.05	7.70
2,500–49,999	6.30	5.82	7.03	6.66	7.91	7.33
Under 2,500	6.11	5.61	7.01	6.41	7.69	7.24

NATIONAL LADDER RATINGS
BY DEMOGRAPHIC GROUPS

	Past		Present		Future	
	1964	1971	1964	1971	1964	1971
NATIONAL	6.12	6.19	6.50	5.38	7.68	6.20
Sex						
Men	6.23	6.22	6.68	5.46	7.74	6.24
Women	6.03	6.14	6.33	5.30	7.62	6.16
Race						
White	6.26	6.26	6.48	5.35	7.53	6.17
Nonwhite	4.89	5.26	6.62	5.81	8.97	6.53
Education						
College	6.12	5.97	6.14	5.39	7.04	6.30
High school	6.14	6.27	6.44	5.38	7.69	6.18
Grade school	6.12	6.20	6.81	5.41	8.06	6.14
Occupation						
Prof. & bus.	6.22	6.06	6.35	5.35	7.37	6.35
White collar	6.10	6.29	6.43	5.36	7.64	6.20
Farmers	6.68	6.12	6.40	5.63	6.93	6.42
Manual	5.92	6.18	6.59	5.34	7.98	6.14
Nonlabor force	6.34	6.30	6.53	5.33	7.58	5.91
Age						
21–29 years	5.91	5.69	6.33	5.06	7.46	6.04
30–49 years	5.99	6.18	6.54	5.43	7.81	6.32
50 & over	6.36	6.46	6.50	5.51	7.57	6.17
Politics						
Republican	6.83	6.23	6.07	5.63	6.98	6.61
Democrat	5.75	6.26	6.89	5.30	8.29	6.12
Independent	6.12	6.07	6.08	5.25	7.06	5.91
Region						
East	6.01	6.18	6.84	5.26	8.07	6.49
Midwest	6.22	6.32	6.49	5.48	7.61	6.20
South	6.22	6.04	6.27	5.46	7.39	5.97
West	5.99	6.18	6.30	5.30	7.55	6.02
Income						
Upper	6.39	6.26	6.50	5.46	7.47	6.47
Upper middle	6.06	6.14	6.51	5.28	7.65	6.10
Lower middle	6.15	6.33	6.63	5.63	7.79	6.51
Lower	5.98	6.10	6.31	5.31	7.81	6.03
Community Size						
500,000 & over	5.85	6.09	6.63	5.17	7.92	6.21
50,000–499,999	6.05	6.38	6.67	5.53	7.90	6.27
2,500–49,999	6.36	6.05	6.39	5.65	7.74	6.48
Under 2,500	6.38	6.22	6.26	5.36	7.16	5.94
Nixon Job Rating						
Approve		6.21		5.65		6.49
Disapprove		6.08		4.93		5.80

TABLE A-7 OPINION ABOUT NATIONAL UNREST by percent

QUESTION: There has been a lot of talk in the news recently about unrest in our country and ill-feeling between groups. In general, how concerned are you about this unrest and ill-feeling? Do you think it is likely to lead to a real breakdown in this country or do you think it is likely to blow over soon?

	real breakdown	blow over soon	don't know
NATIONAL	47	38	15
Sex			
Men	45	42	13
Women	48	35	17
Race			
White	47	39	14
Nonwhite	40	33	27
Education			
College	49	34	17
High school	49	39	12
Grade school	38	41	21
Occupation			
Prof. & bus.	46	38	16
White collar	59	29	12
Farmers	52	34	14
Manual	47	38	15
Nonlabor force	41	41	18
Age			
21–29 years	57	30	13
30–49 years	51	35	14
50 & over	37	45	18
Politics			
Republican	42	45	13
Democrat	45	37	18
Independent	53	35	12
Region			
East	44	39	17
Midwest	48	39	13
South	48	36	16
West	48	37	15
Income			
$15,000 & over	45	40	15
$7,000–$14,999	49	39	12
$5,000–$6,999	48	37	15
Under $5,000	41	38	21

	real breakdown	blow over soon	don't know
Community Size			
500,000 & over	46	35	19
50,000–499,999	44	43	13
2,500–49,999	50	36	14
Under 2,500	48	38	14
Nixon Job Rating			
Approve	43	44	13
Disapprove	54	33	13

QUESTION: All things considered, which one or two of the reasons listed on this card do you think are mainly responsible for this unrest and ill-feeling between groups?

A. Our traditional way of doing things is not working and some basic changes are needed if we are to work together.

B. Some Negroes and other minorities are making unreasonable demands.

C. Many of the problems our country faces are so big that we can't agree on how to solve them.

D. The protests are largely communist inspired.

E. Our leaders in government and business are not trying hard enough to solve the problems we face and people are losing confidence in them.

F. Some young people have gotten out of hand and have no respect for authority.

	A	B	C	D	E	F	don't know
NATIONAL	34	31	19	31	31	32	7
Sex							
Men	32	34	16	29	33	33	6
Women	36	28	21	33	29	32	7
Race							
White	34	32	18	32	30	33	6
Nonwhite	39	14	22	20	42	24	13
Education							
College	53	21	27	20	35	21	5
High school	31	34	17	35	30	34	7
Grade school	23	34	16	34	28	40	9
Occupation							
Prof. & bus.	48	26	23	27	32	27	5
White collar	40	28	17	37	27	32	4
Farmers	23	33	17	41	30	37	9
Manual	31	31	18	33	31	32	7
Nonlabor force	28	34	17	29	32	39	8
Age							
21–29 years	46	23	23	22	39	22	5
30–49 years	38	30	20	31	28	31	6
50 & over	25	35	16	36	29	39	9

	A	B	C	D	E	F	don't know
Politics							
Republican	31	33	18	38	22	37	5
Democrat	33	31	20	30	31	34	8
Independent	40	29	19	28	36	27	5
Region							
East	39	30	20	28	32	32	6
Midwest	29	32	18	31	30	34	7
South	30	35	18	35	30	30	9
West	42	22	20	31	32	32	4
Income							
$15,000 & over	40	25	21	32	29	27	5
$7,000–$14,999	37	34	18	30	32	32	6
$5,000–$6,999	38	26	17	27	34	32	5
Under $5,000	27	30	18	33	29	36	9
Community Size							
500,000 & over	39	28	21	29	31	29	8
50,000–499,999	36	28	17	33	34	32	5
2,500–49,999	32	37	17	27	26	35	7
Under 2,500	29	32	18	35	30	34	6
Nixon Job Rating							
Approve	31	32	18	38	24	37	5
Disapprove	40	27	20	23	42	27	7
Concern Over Unrest							
Real breakdown	36	31	19	33	34	31	4
Blow over soon	32	32	18	33	28	35	5

QUESTION: There are a number of issues people have been protesting and demonstrating about. Which one or two of the issues listed on this card do you, yourself, think most of this protest has been about?

A. The war in Vietnam
B. Discrimination against minorities and inequality between the races
C. Dissatisfaction with our system of government and the business establishment
D. The impatience of young people with the views of older people
E. The danger of nuclear war
F. Lack of trust in most of the individuals in positions of leadership

	A	B	C	D	E	F	don't know
NATIONAL	66	37	20	24	6	23	5
Sex							
Men	65	35	20	25	5	25	4
Women	67	40	20	22	7	22	5
Race							
White	67	36	20	24	6	24	4
Nonwhite	54	51	18	20	4	19	10
Education							
College	72	41	26	18	3	24	2
High school	70	38	19	23	6	21	4
Grade school	52	34	16	29	9	27	8
Occupation							
Prof. & bus.	73	40	24	21	5	23	4
White collar	78	50	15	18	3	14	5
Farmers	62	34	15	33	5	29	4
Manual	65	38	21	21	6	24	4
Nonlabor force	57	29	19	30	9	26	9
Age							
21–29 years	77	47	25	13	5	19	3
30–49 years	68	41	21	22	5	23	3
50 & over	59	30	17	31	8	26	7
Politics							
Republican	69	37	18	26	5	22	4
Democrat	65	36	19	25	7	23	6
Independent	64	39	24	19	5	26	4

	A	B	C	D	E	F	don't know
Region							
East	69	35	23	23	5	25	5
Midwest	66	36	17	23	6	24	5
South	61	44	13	27	7	20	6
West	68	35	30	20	7	25	2
Income							
$15,000 & over	74	37	21	19	3	23	3
$7,000–$14,999	70	41	18	24	5	26	2
$5,000–$6,999	68	36	24	21	7	21	3
Under $5,000	57	32	18	26	9	21	10
Community Size							
500,000 & over	69	39	22	22	7	23	6
50,000–499,999	70	39	24	26	5	20	2
2,500–49,999	60	37	13	22	7	24	8
Under 2,500	63	35	18	25	6	26	5
Nixon Job Rating							
Approve	66	37	19	28	5	21	3
Disapprove	70	40	23	19	7	26	3
Concern Over Unrest							
Real breakdown	66	39	23	21	6	27	3
Blow over soon	70	36	18	29	6	19	2

QUESTION: *Suppose the United States were confronted with a choice of only the two alternatives listed on this card, which one would you rather have the United States follow?*

A. End the war by accepting the best possible compromise settlement even though it might sooner or later allow the Vietnamese communists to take over control of South Vietnam

B. Fight on until a settlement can be reached which will insure that the communists do not get control of South Vietnam

	end war	fight on	don't know
NATIONAL	55	36	9
Sex			
Men	52	40	8
Women	57	33	10
Race			
White	53	38	9
Nonwhite	73	13	14
Education			
College	60	35	5
High school	52	39	9
Grade school	55	30	15
Occupation			
Prof. & bus.	59	35	6
White collar	61	32	7
Farmers	47	38	15
Manual	48	42	10
Nonlabor force	61	27	12
Age			
21–29 years	61	35	4
30–49 years	51	40	9
50 & over	55	33	12
Politics			
Republican	56	39	5
Democrat	54	36	10
Independent	55	34	11

	end war	fight on	don't know
Region			
East	61	31	8
Midwest	49	41	10
South	51	39	10
West	59	33	8
Income			
$15,000 & over	61	34	5
$7,000–$14,999	47	45	8
$5,000–$6,999	62	32	6
Under $5,000	60	25	15
Community Size			
500,000 & over	60	32	8
50,000–499,999	57	38	5
2,500–49,999	51	38	11
Under 2,500	49	38	13
Nixon Job Rating			
Approve	49	44	7
Disapprove	63	29	8

TABLE A-11 GREATEST CONCERN IF US VIETNAM EFFORT FAILED by percent

QUESTION: Thinking about all that the United States has done over the years to help the South Vietnamese fight the war, suppose that the entire effort failed as the United States continued to withdraw its troops. Which of these things would really bother you the most—that the communists would be expanding their influence by taking over one more country, or that we had been defeated in Vietnam, losing our first war in this century?

	communist gain	US defeat	both, neither	don't know
NATIONAL	58	18	13	11
Sex				
Men	52	22	17	9
Women	62	15	10	13
Race				
White	59	18	13	10
Nonwhite	45	25	6	24
Education				
College	66	14	16	4
High school	61	18	11	10
Grade school	42	23	15	20
Occupation				
Prof. & bus.	62	17	17	4
White collar	64	16	9	11
Farmers	59	20	5	16
Manual	59	18	12	11
Nonlabor force	45	21	14	20
Age				
21–29 years	69	14	10	7
30–49 years	61	18	13	8
50 & over	48	20	15	17
Politics				
Republican	58	21	12	9
Democrat	57	18	12	13
Independent	58	16	15	11
Region				
East	53	21	14	12
Midwest	58	19	13	10
South	58	19	10	13
West	65	10	17	8

	communist gain	US defeat	both, neither	don't know
Income				
$15,000 & over	63	16	16	5
$7,000–$14,999	65	18	11	6
$5,000–$6,999	57	15	12	16
Under $5,000	44	21	15	20
Community Size				
500,000 & over	55	19	13	13
50,000–499,999	64	12	15	9
2,500–49,999	55	23	13	9
Under 2,500	56	19	11	14
Nixon Job Rating				
Approve	63	19	11	7
Disapprove	55	18	15	12
Attitude Toward War				
End war	53	18	16	13
Fight on	69	19	8	4

QUESTION: *Please read the statement on this card. Do you agree or disagree with it?*

We shouldn't think so much in **international** terms but concentrate more on our own **national** problems and building up our strength and prosperity here at home.

	agree	disagree	don't know
NATIONAL	77	16	7
Sex			
Men	76	18	6
Women	79	14	7
Race			
White	77	17	6
Nonwhite	84	4	12
Education			
College	66	27	7
High school	79	14	7
Grade school	85	9	6
Occupation			
Prof. & bus.	69	24	7
White collar	80	15	5
Farmers	79	11	10
Manual	78	17	5
Nonlabor force	82	9	9
Age			
21–29 years	79	17	4
30–49 years	73	21	6
50 & over	81	11	8
Politics			
Republican	75	19	6
Democrat	80	13	7
Independent	77	16	7
Region			
East	79	14	7
Midwest	74	18	8
South	76	17	7
West	80	15	5

	agree	disagree	don't know
Income			
$15,000 & over	64	28	8
$7,000–$14,999	77	18	5
$5,000–$6,999	83	10	7
Under $5,000	83	10	7
Community Size			
500,000 & over	75	18	7
50,000–499,999	75	21	4
2,500–49,999	72	17	11
Under 2,500	83	10	7
Nixon Job Rating			
Approve	73	20	7
Disapprove	82	13	5

QUESTION: On the whole, do you think that the chances of a major world war breaking out have increased or decreased in recent years?

	increased	decreased	about the same	don't know
NATIONAL	46	33	12	9
Sex				
Men	42	40	12	6
Women	48	28	12	12
Race				
White	45	34	12	9
Nonwhite	57	23	6	14
Education				
College	32	52	11	5
High school	49	31	12	8
Grade school	52	19	13	16
Occupation				
Prof. & bus.	36	50	10	4
White collar	47	31	13	9
Farmers	52	28	9	11
Manual	51	29	12	8
Nonlabor force	43	24	15	18
Age				
21–29 years	53	35	7	5
30–49 years	43	40	11	6
50 & over	44	26	15	15
Politics				
Republican	41	37	14	8
Democrat	48	30	11	11
Independent	46	35	11	8
Region				
East	40	35	14	11
Midwest	44	34	14	8
South	52	29	7	12
West	48	35	13	4

	increased	decreased	about the same	don't know
Income				
$15,000 & over	35	49	10	6
$7,000–$14,999	45	39	11	5
$5,000–$6,999	51	26	11	12
Under $5,000	48	21	15	16
Community Size				
500,000 & over	48	33	10	9
50,000–499,999	44	39	10	7
2,500–49,999	48	29	10	13
Under 2,500	49	30	12	9

TABLE A-14 REASONS WAR MAY BE LESS LIKELY by percent

QUESTION: Which one or two of the reasons listed on this card do you, yourself, think has made it **less** likely that a major world war will break out? (Asked only of those believing chances of a major war have decreased.)

A. America has learned a lesson from Vietnam and will not be so quick to become involved in similar situations in the future.
B. The United States is strong enough to keep other nations from risking war.
C. The Russians now feel that it is in their own interest to be more cooperative and work for world peace.
D. Communist China has been so busy dealing with its own internal problems that it has become less aggressive.
E. The Russians and the Chinese are no longer working together and are not the combined threat they used to be.
F. The poor and backward nations of the world are making enough progress so that there are fewer reasons for local conflicts to be blown up into world problems.
G. People everywhere are tired of war and there are new kinds of international cooperation that are becoming more and more important.

	A	B	C	D	E	F	G	none of these	don't know
NATIONAL	11	9	12	2	7	2	14	1	1
Sex									
Men	12	13	15	2	9	2	14	1	1
Women	10	5	8	2	5	1	15	1	1
Race									
White	11	9	12	2	7	2	14	1	1
Nonwhite	12	7	4	—	2	2	17	—	2
Education									
College	14	11	24	3	13	1	21	2	1
High school	9	9	10	1	6	3	13	1	1
Grade school	11	6	2	1	3	1	9	—	2
Occupation									
Prof. & bus.	15	14	23	3	9	3	21	1	—
White collar	9	10	9	1	11	—	13	—	1
Farmers	10	9	6	2	2	3	12	2	—
Manual	10	8	9	1	5	2	13	1	1
Nonlabor force	9	4	6	1	6	1	11	—	3

	A	B	C	D	E	F	G	none of these	don't know
Age									
21–29 years	9	7	16	2	9	1	16	1	—
30–49 years	12	11	13	3	9	2	18	1	1
50 & over	11	8	8	1	4	1	10	1	2
Politics									
Republican	12	10	12	2	9	2	15	1	1
Democrat	10	7	9	1	5	2	12	1	2
Independent	10	10	14	2	7	1	16	1	—
Region									
East	12	9	14	1	7	3	15	1	1
Midwest	11	9	13	1	6	2	13	1	1
South	10	9	6	2	6	1	13	2	2
West	11	8	14	3	9	1	17	—	—
Income									
$15,000 & over	13	11	23	3	13	2	20	1	1
$7,000–$14,999	11	11	15	2	8	2	16	1	1
$5,000–$6,999	12	8	6	1	4	2	11	1	1
Under $5,000	9	6	4	1	4	2	11	1	2
Community Size									
500,000 & over	11	7	13	2	7	1	15	1	2
50,000–499,999	16	12	14	2	7	3	17	1	—
2,500–49,999	8	6	10	1	7	2	13	1	2
Under 2,500	8	10	9	2	6	2	13	1	1
Nixon Job Rating									
Approve	11	12	12	2	8	2	15	1	1
Disapprove	12	6	13	1	7	2	16	1	1
Problem Emphasis									
National	11	8	11	1	6	2	14	1	1
International	12	11	14	4	10	1	16	—	1

TABLE A-15 REASONS WAR MAY BE MORE LIKELY by percent

QUESTION: Which one or two of the reasons listed on this card do you, yourself, think has made it **more** likely that a major world war will break out? (Asked only of those believing chances of a major war have increased.)

A. The difficulties the United States has had in Vietnam will encourage the communists to cause trouble elsewhere in the world.

B. The United States has cut back on its military defenses and is not as able to deal with any threat as it was.

C. The Russians have always been aggressive and they will always try to expand their influence.

D. Communist China is still working hard to cause trouble in Asia and will try to spread its influence throughout the world regardless of the cost in human lives.

E. Regardless of what people say, Russia and China are allies and will continue to work together, especially when the going gets tough.

F. The poor and backward nations of the world are so weak that there is always the chance that some local conflict will be blown up into a world problem.

G. Even though people may be tired of war and want peace, there will always be sources of conflict that the major powers will not be able to keep from turning into larger wars.

	A	B	C	D	E	F	G	none of these	don't know
NATIONAL	12	5	13	15	8	7	15	1	2
Sex									
Men	11	6	13	13	7	7	12	2	1
Women	13	4	14	16	9	7	17	1	2
Race									
White	12	5	14	14	8	7	15	1	2
Nonwhite	16	6	9	18	9	10	19	1	6
Education									
College	7	3	8	13	5	5	13	1	1
High school	13	5	15	15	10	8	17	1	1
Grade school	14	7	15	14	9	6	12	2	5

	A	B	C	D	E	F	G	none of these	don't know
Occupation									
Prof. & bus.	10	2	8	13	8	5	11	1	1
White collar	10	6	16	13	7	9	17	1	1
Farmers	13	9	15	16	13	12	12	—	—
Manual	13	5	14	18	9	7	18	2	3
Nonlabor force	12	7	15	11	7	7	13	1	2
Age									
21–29 years	11	4	13	18	5	8	21	4	2
30–49 years	12	4	10	15	9	7	15	1	1
50 & over	13	6	17	13	10	7	11	1	3
Politics									
Republican	12	8	13	14	5	5	11	—	2
Democrat	13	4	14	14	11	7	16	2	2
Independent	11	4	12	15	8	9	16	2	1
Region									
East	10	4	9	12	8	5	13	1	2
Midwest	12	5	14	13	6	7	14	2	2
South	14	7	14	18	12	8	16	1	3
West	13	4	18	18	7	9	15	1	1
Income									
$15,000 & over	7	2	9	13	6	5	11	1	1
$7,000–$14,999	12	5	13	16	9	6	15	1	1
$5,000–$6,999	14	5	15	14	7	9	17	2	3
Under $5,000	13	6	16	13	8	7	14	1	4
Community Size									
500,000 & over	12	6	10	13	8	6	15	1	1
50,000–499,999	11	4	15	14	8	6	14	1	2
2,500–49,999	13	5	16	16	10	5	16	1	3
Under 2,500	13	5	14	16	9	9	15	2	2
Nixon Job Rating									
Approve	12	5	13	15	9	6	13	—	2
Disapprove	12	6	14	14	9	8	16	3	2
Problem Emphasis									
National	13	5	14	14	9	7	16	1	2
International	12	5	11	17	9	7	14	2	—

US RESPONSE TO ATTACK ON SPECIFIC NATIONS
by percent

QUESTION: In the event a nation is attacked by communist-backed forces, there are several things the Unit
States can do about it. As I read the name of each country, tell me what action you would want to see us take
if that nation is actually attacked—send American troops or send military supplies but not send American troo
or refuse to get involved at all.

	West Germany				Turkey				Israel			
	send troops	send supplies only	refuse to get involved	don't know	send troops	send supplies only	refuse to get involved	don't know	send troops	send supplies only	refuse to get involved	don kno
NATIONAL	28	41	22	9	10	36	37	17	11	44	33	12
Sex												
Men	35	40	17	8	14	40	33	13	14	47	29	10
Women	21	42	26	11	7	32	40	21	10	41	36	13
Race												
White	29	42	20	9	10	37	37	16	12	45	32	11
Nonwhite	11	32	42	15	6	24	44	26	11	29	40	20
Education												
College	36	45	12	7	11	44	35	10	13	53	27	7
High school	28	41	22	9	11	35	36	18	13	43	32	12
Grade school	17	37	33	13	6	30	40	24	7	37	40	16
Occupation												
Prof. & bus.	35	46	13	6	9	46	36	9	12	50	31	7
White collar	27	41	24	8	9	39	38	14	11	43	34	12
Farmers	22	35	23	20	6	32	38	24	3	35	41	21
Manual	31	39	22	8	14	35	32	19	15	45	30	10
Nonlabor force	16	40	31	13	4	25	49	22	6	40	37	17
Age												
21–29 years	33	45	18	4	13	46	29	12	14	50	29	7
30–49 years	32	41	19	8	14	37	34	15	15	45	30	10
50 & over	20	40	27	13	5	29	44	22	6	40	37	17
Politics												
Republican	32	39	21	8	9	37	39	15	10	47	32	11
Democrat	26	42	23	9	9	36	36	19	12	43	33	12
Independent	26	43	20	11	13	36	34	17	12	45	31	12
Region												
East	27	39	25	9	9	36	41	14	13	47	28	12
Midwest	29	39	22	10	9	35	38	18	11	40	36	1
South	26	42	22	10	10	34	34	22	12	40	34	14
West	29	47	17	7	13	39	34	14	9	51	34	6
Income												
$15,000 & over	38	43	12	7	13	47	32	8	12	51	30	7
$7,000–$14,999	32	42	18	8	10	38	36	16	13	48	29	10
$5,000–$6,999	24	45	21	10	12	34	35	19	12	43	31	14
Under $5,000	16	38	33	13	7	27	43	23	9	35	40	16
Community Size												
500,000 & over	26	41	25	8	10	37	39	14	11	46	32	11
50,000–499,999	30	42	20	8	14	39	33	14	14	47	31	8
2,500–49,999	32	39	20	9	9	33	41	17	13	39	35	1
Under 2,500	24	42	22	12	8	33	36	23	9	42	33	16
Nixon Job Rating												
Approve	32	41	17	10	12	38	32	18	13	46	29	12
Disapprove	25	43	25	7	8	36	43	13	10	45	36	
Problem Emphasis												
National	23	43	25	9	8	34	42	16	9	44	36	1
International	49	34	8	9	24	42	21	13	20	47	23	10

	Japan				England				India			
	send troops	send supplies only	refuse to get involved	don't know	send troops	send supplies only	refuse to get involved	don't know	send troops	send supplies only	refuse to get involved	don't know
NATIONAL	17	34	38	11	37	33	19	11	7	40	39	14
Sex												
Men	22	37	33	8	44	29	17	10	8	41	38	13
Women	11	32	44	13	31	36	22	11	7	39	39	15
Race												
White	17	35	38	10	39	33	18	10	8	40	38	14
Nonwhite	10	22	49	19	19	22	38	21	5	35	43	17
Education												
College	23	42	29	6	49	33	13	5	7	48	37	8
High school	16	33	40	11	38	33	18	11	9	40	37	14
Grade school	11	29	44	16	24	31	29	16	5	33	43	19
Occupation												
Prof. & bus.	20	42	34	4	48	34	13	5	5	51	36	8
White collar	23	29	37	11	38	34	17	11	13	41	36	10
Farmers	8	22	48	22	20	33	28	19	6	30	41	23
Manual	20	35	35	10	42	29	19	10	10	42	35	13
Nonlabor force	6	29	49	16	20	36	27	17	3	28	48	21
Age												
21–29 years	23	41	29	7	51	28	15	6	13	50	30	7
30–49 years	20	37	33	10	44	32	15	9	8	44	35	13
50 & over	9	29	48	14	24	35	26	15	3	32	46	19
Politics												
Republican	18	31	41	10	40	32	18	10	6	40	41	13
Democrat	15	35	39	11	35	32	22	11	7	39	39	15
Independent	18	36	35	11	40	33	15	12	9	43	35	13
Region												
East	14	35	43	8	34	36	20	10	8	40	40	12
Midwest	17	33	37	13	36	32	20	12	6	40	38	16
South	17	30	39	14	39	25	22	14	9	33	41	17
West	19	42	32	7	42	39	14	5	5	51	35	9
Income												
$15,000 & over	21	41	32	6	50	30	14	6	9	44	36	11
$7,000–$14,999	19	38	35	8	44	33	15	8	8	46	35	11
$5,000–$6,999	16	33	36	15	34	34	19	13	6	43	35	16
Under $5,000	11	25	48	16	23	31	30	16	6	28	47	19
Community Size												
500,000 & over	16	36	37	11	35	35	19	11	6	43	38	13
50,000–499,999	19	37	37	7	43	31	18	8	11	45	35	9
2,500–49,999	15	32	41	12	37	33	20	10	5	36	44	15
Under 2,500	16	31	39	14	35	30	21	14	6	35	39	20
Nixon Job Rating												
Approve	18	37	34	11	42	34	13	11	8	43	34	15
Disapprove	15	35	42	8	34	34	24	8	7	40	43	10
Problem Emphasis												
National	14	33	43	10	34	34	22	10	5	40	42	13
International	29	42	21	8	54	26	10	10	18	44	27	11

	Mexico				Thailand				Brazil			
	send troops	send sup-plies only	refuse to get in-volved	don't know	send troops	send sup-plies only	refuse to get in-volved	don't know	send troops	send sup-plies only	refuse to get in-volved	don't know
NATIONAL	45	26	19	10	11	36	38	15	16	36	33	15
Sex												
Men	53	23	15	9	13	37	36	14	20	39	28	13
Women	39	28	23	10	9	36	39	16	12	34	37	17
Race												
White	47	26	17	10	12	37	37	14	16	37	32	15
Nonwhite	26	26	37	11	4	29	41	26	7	32	41	20
Education												
College	55	28	11	6	11	45	36	8	18	46	28	8
High school	46	24	19	11	13	35	36	16	17	36	32	15
Grade school	33	27	28	12	7	30	42	21	10	29	40	21
Occupation												
Prof. & bus.	55	28	10	7	11	45	35	9	17	50	24	9
White collar	49	25	16	10	15	36	36	13	17	39	29	15
Farmers	42	20	27	11	5	33	38	24	11	31	39	19
Manual	46	24	20	10	15	36	33	16	20	33	32	15
Nonlabor force	34	25	27	14	3	27	50	20	6	29	45	20
Age												
21–29 years	52	25	14	9	17	43	30	10	22	41	27	10
30–49 years	52	24	15	9	13	41	34	12	18	41	27	14
50 & over	36	27	25	12	6	29	44	21	10	30	41	19
Politics												
Republican	49	25	19	7	10	38	38	14	15	38	34	13
Democrat	44	25	21	10	11	36	37	16	14	36	33	17
Independent	44	27	16	13	12	36	37	15	18	37	32	13
Region												
East	37	30	22	11	11	36	42	11	15	39	34	12
Midwest	52	22	16	10	8	35	40	17	16	35	31	18
South	45	21	20	14	14	36	31	19	18	33	31	18
West	48	30	18	4	12	40	38	10	13	40	36	11
Income												
$15,000 & over	57	26	10	7	15	43	31	11	18	46	26	10
$7,000–$14,999	52	25	15	8	11	41	35	13	18	41	28	13
$5,000–$6,999	44	28	18	10	12	35	38	15	16	34	32	18
Under $5,000	28	25	32	15	7	26	46	21	9	26	44	21
Community Size												
500,000 & over	41	29	20	10	11	37	40	12	14	40	33	13
50,000–499,999	48	25	19	8	15	38	37	10	17	40	32	11
2,500–49,999	48	25	18	9	11	35	39	15	15	35	35	15
Under 2,500	46	23	19	12	8	35	35	22	16	32	32	20
Nixon Job Rating												
Approve	51	24	15	10	13	40	32	15	19	39	27	15
Disapprove	40	29	22	9	9	34	46	11	14	35	39	12
Problem Emphasis												
National	42	27	22	9	9	36	42	13	13	37	37	13
International	63	21	6	10	24	44	19	13	30	39	18	13

	Yugoslavia				Nationalist China			
	send troops	send supplies only	refuse to get involved	don't know	send troops	send supplies only	refuse to get involved	don't know
NATIONAL	7	27	51	15	11	30	45	14
Sex								
Men	8	27	52	13	13	34	41	12
Women	6	27	50	17	8	28	48	16
Race								
White	7	28	51	14	11	32	44	13
Nonwhite	5	21	49	25	6	21	52	21
Education								
College	7	29	52	12	11	38	42	9
High school	8	27	51	14	12	30	45	13
Grade school	4	25	50	21	8	25	47	20
Occupation								
Prof. & bus.	7	34	49	10	13	38	40	9
White collar	9	26	54	11	12	28	51	9
Farmers	2	19	56	23	9	17	49	25
Manual	9	27	49	15	13	30	44	13
Nonlabor force	3	21	55	21	3	28	49	20
Age								
–29 years	10	30	50	10	13	35	44	8
30–49 years	7	31	49	13	15	32	41	12
50 & over	4	23	53	20	5	27	49	19
Politics								
Republican	5	27	53	15	11	34	42	13
Democrat	7	29	47	17	10	30	44	16
Independent	8	27	52	13	12	28	48	12
Region								
East	6	30	52	12	10	31	47	12
Midwest	6	26	51	17	10	27	47	16
South	9	23	48	20	13	28	41	18
West	6	31	52	11	8	41	43	8
Income								
$15,000 & over	8	33	49	10	12	37	43	8
$10,000–$14,999	8	28	51	13	12	34	42	12
$7,000–$6,999	5	27	51	17	10	30	46	14
Under $5,000	5	22	50	23	6	23	50	21
Community Size								
500,000 & over	7	31	49	13	11	32	46	11
100,000–499,999	10	30	49	11	13	36	40	11
50,000–49,999	7	19	57	17	10	28	47	15
Under 2,500	5	25	49	21	8	26	19	47
Nixon Job Rating								
Approve	7	30	47	16	13	33	39	15
Disapprove	6	27	55	12	9	31	49	11
Problem Emphasis								
National	6	27	54	13	8	30	50	12
International	14	31	41	14	23	35	29	13

Appendix 2 Design and composition of the samples

The Gallup Organization, which designed the samples upon which this study is based, maintains a national probability sample of interviewing areas that is used for all National Opinion Trends surveys. The sampling procedure is designed to produce an approximation of the adult civilian population, twenty-one years and older, living in the United States, except for those persons in institutions such as prisons or hospitals.

The design of the sample is that of a replicated, probability sample, down to the block level in the case of urban areas and to segments of townships in the case of rural areas. Approximately three hundred sampling points—clusters of blocks or rural segments—were used in each survey.

The sample design included stratification by these seven size-of-community strata: central cities with a population of 1 million and over; of 250,000 to 999,999; of 50,000 to 249,999; the urbanized areas of all these central cities as a single stratum; cities 2,500 to 49,999; rural villages; rural open areas. Each of these strata was further stratified into seven geographic regions. Within each city-size regional stratum, the population was geographically ordered and zoned into equal sized groups of sampling units. Pairs of localities were then randomly selected in each zone, producing two replicated samples of localities.

Within the localities selected for which population data were available, subdivisions were drawn with the probability of selection proportional to size of population. In all other localities, small definable geographic areas were selected with equal probability. Within each subdivision selected for which block statistics were available, a sample of blocks was drawn with probability of selection proportional to the number of dwelling units. In all other subdivisions or areas, blocks or segments were drawn at random.

In each cluster of selected blocks or segments, a randomly selected starting point was designated on the interviewer's map of the area. Starting at this point, the interviewer followed a specified direction in the selection of households until he completed his assignment. Interviewing was conducted at times when adults in general were most likely to be at home—on weekends or on weekdays after 4:00 P.M. for women and after 6:00 P.M. for men.

Allowance for persons not at home was made by a "times-at-home" technique rather than by "call-backs." This procedure is a standard method for reducing the sample bias that would otherwise result from under-representation of those who are difficult to find at home.

The prestratification by regions was supplemented by fitting each obtained sample to the latest available Census Bureau estimates of the regional distribution of the population. Also, minor adjustments of the sample were made by educational attainment (for men and women separately), based on the annual estimates of the Census Bureau derived from their Current Population Survey.

The composition of the samples appears in table A-17.

TABLE A-17 COMPOSITION OF THE SAMPLES

	January, 1971		April, 1971	
	no. of interviews	% of sample (weighted)	no. of interviews	% of sample (weighted)
NATIONAL TOTAL	1588	100.0	1446	100.0
Sex				
Men	777	47.9	692	46.5
Women	811	52.1	754	53.5
Race				
White	1449	90.9	1327	91.0
Negro	124	8.0	107	8.1
Other	15	1.1	12	0.9
Education				
College	447	23.4	401	23.9
High school	861	52.0	729	51.7
Grade school	275	24.4	309	24.2
Undesignated	5	0.2	7	0.2
Occupation of Head of Household				
Prof. & bus.	387	21.7	345	23.1
White collar	187	11.4	135	9.2
Farmers	92	6.1	81	5.7
Manual	611	40.2	549	39.3
Nonlabor force	287	19.2	307	20.6
Undesignated	24	1.4	29	2.1
Age				
21–29 years	343	21.6	301	21.1
30–49 years	571	35.2	540	37.6
50 years & over	660	42.4	596	40.6
Undesignated	14	0.8	9	0.7
Religion				
Protestant	1001	63.7	922	62.3
Catholic	441	27.2	372	27.0
Jewish	47	2.8	41	2.9
All others	99	6.3	111	7.8
Political Affiliation				
Republican	471	28.9	401	26.4
Democrat	647	41.6	596	41.3
Independent	435	27.3	408	29.1
All others	35	2.2	41	3.2

	January, 1971		April, 1971	
	no. of interviews	% of sample (weighted)	no. of interviews	% of sample (weighted)
Region				
East	468	29.4	404	28.3
Midwest	470	28.1	431	28.1
South	406	26.2	362	26.7
West	244	16.3	249	16.9
Household Income				
$15,000 and over	253	14.4	234	15.1
$7,000–$14,999	715	44.0	592	40.9
$5,000–$6,999	249	16.2	190	13.5
Under $5,000	350	24.2	369	26.2
Undesignated	21	1.2	61	4.3
Community Size				
500,000 and over	538	33.8	449	31.5
50,000–499,999	369	22.6	345	23.8
2,500–4,999	262	15.7	227	15.3
Under 2,500	419	27.9	425	29.4